The Psychology of Cricket

Developing Mental Toughness

Dr. Stewart Cotterill

Dr. Jamie Barker

BENNION
KEARNY

Published in 2013 by Bennion Kearny Limited.

Copyright © Bennion Kearny Ltd 2013

ISBN: 978-1-909125-21-6

Published by Bennion Kearny Limited
6 Victory House
64 Trafalgar Road
Birmingham
B13 8BU

www.BennionKearny.com

Cover image: Shutterstock/albund

To my daughter Isabelle, always follow your dreams.

- Stewart -

For Emma, Lucy, Mum and Dad, with all my love.

- Jamie -

Acknowledgements

Stewart Cotterill: This book has been a few years in development and for me stemmed from discussions with Jason Kerr and Andy Hurry at Somerset County Cricket Club. So, I would like to thank both of them for lighting the fuse. I would like to thank the members of the County Cricket Sport Psychology network in the United Kingdom (UK) for helping in discussing appropriate approaches and techniques for working with cricketers. To all the cricket coaches and players I have worked with over the years, thank you for the experience and knowledge you have offered me. Finally to the England and Wales Cricket Board's (ECB) Performance Programme (EPP) and Performance Psychology team for the experiences, support and development they have afforded me.

I would like to thank my Dad, Tom, for igniting a passion and appreciation for cricket in me at an early age, and to my wife, Karen, and daughter, Isabelle, for just being you.

Jamie Barker: For many years I have wanted to write this book to enable players, coaches, and parents to maximise cricket performance based on my work and experiences in professional cricket. First and foremost, I would like to thank three of my colleagues - Andrew Evans, Matthew Slater, and Martin Turner for their significant contributions in chapters two, four, and seven and overall assistance in helping compile this book. They are three of the most capable, motivated, and creative individuals I have had the pleasure of working with. The 'future' of sport psychology is in safe hands. Second, I would like to thank all of the county coaches, players, and sport psychologists whom I have worked with, along with the support staff at the England and Wales Cricket Board (ECB). You have always shared your thoughts and experiences and supported me in my work. Third, I am indebted to my parents (Linda and Roger) for giving me the love of a wonderful game, buying me my first bat and ball, the hours of practice, the endless 'taxi' rides, and the confidence to have no regrets. Finally, I owe everything to the endless patience, support, and love of my wife, Emma, and my daughter, Lucy. My girls are my world.

About the Authors

Dr. Stewart Cotterill is an applied sport psychology consultant with over 12 years of experience working in both Professional and Amateur sports. He is a Chartered member of the British Psychological Society and a HCPC Registered Sport and Exercise Psychologist in the UK. He currently runs his own Performance Psychology Consultancy business called Performance Mind (www.performancemind.co.uk) and is also employed as a Senior Lecturer in Sport Psychology at the University of Winchester, United Kingdom (www.winchester.ac.uk). Stewart's experience in cricket ranges from working with amateur players, University players, professional clubs and as part of an international team development programme.

Dr. Jamie Barker is a Senior Lecturer in Sport and Exercise Psychology at Staffordshire University, UK. (www.staffs.ac.uk/research/csher/index.jsp). He is a Chartered Psychologist with the British Psychological Society (BPS), a registered Sport and Exercise Psychologist with the Health and Care Professions Council (HCPC), and a British Association of Sport and Exercise Sciences (BASES) accredited sport and exercise scientist. He is an active researcher with book authorship, numerous publications in international journals, and chapters in edited books. Jamie is an active consultant with over 14 years of experience working in a variety of professional sports (including soccer and golf) with a major focus in cricket.

About the Contributors

Chapter 2 written in collaboration with Andrew Evans.

Andrew L. Evans, MSc, is a lecturer, researcher, and consultant at the Centre for Sport, Health, and Exercise Research at Staffordshire University. Andrew has provided sport psychology education and support to athletes competing in sports including cricket, equestrianism, ice skating, and volleyball.

*

Chapter 4 written in collaboration with Martin Turner.

Martin J. Turner, MSc, is an HCPC registered sport and exercise psychologist currently researching and lecturing in the Centre for Sport, Health, and Exercise Research at Staffordshire University. Martin specialises in the influence of stress and emotion on performance, and in the use of Rational-Emotive Behavior Therapy with athletes. He currently consults with professional soccer and cricket academies and multinational business corporations.

*

Chapter 7 written in collaboration with Matt Slater.

Matt Slater, MSc, is currently with the Centre for Sport, Health, and Exercise Research at Staffordshire University. He works as a researcher and consultant in professional cricket and football with an interest in leadership and the application of psychological skills in performance settings.

Table of Contents

Start of Play   1

Chapter 1 – The Mental Side of Cricket   3
What is the Mental Game?...4
How Does the Mind Affect Cricket Performance?....................6
Strategies to Become Mentally Stronger 7
Gaining Further Support 9
The Benefits of Working with a Sport Psychologist...............12
Summary 14

Chapter 2 – Being Motivated and Committed in Cricket   15
What is Motivation?...16
The Effects of Motivation on Cricket Performance.................17
Outlook and its Influence on Cricket Motivation 20
Factors Influencing Cricket Motivation..............................23
Enhancing Cricket Motivation 27
Summary 33
Further reading:..34
Advanced reading: 34
Goal Setting Resources 35
Resources. 35

Chapter 3 – Staying Focused   39
What is Focusing?...40
The Effects of Focusing on Cricket 42
Strategies to Enhance Focus 45
Focusing Routines...45
Cue Words...49
Triggers 50
Self-Talk...50
Goal-Setting 51
Summary 52
Further reading:..53
Advanced reading: 53
Resources 54

Chapter 4 – Performing Under Pressure 55

Why can Pressure be so Bad?... 56
Thinking too much 57
Don't mess up! 58
Focusing on the wrong things... 60
Feeling Threatened 61
Thriving Under Pressure.. 64
    Thinking Smart... 64
    'See' yourself cope 67
Focusing on the right things 69
Oh, the irony... 71
    Empty your head.. 71
    Be ironic to fight irony 71
    Adapt 72
Bringing it all together... 73
Feeling challenged... 74
    Self-Confidence... 74
    Control 75
    Approach Focus 75
Summary.. 75
Further reading: 76
Advanced reading:... 76

Chapter 5 – Becoming Mentally Tough 77

What is Mental Toughness? 78
Mental Toughness in Cricket.. 82
Measuring Mental Toughness in Cricket 88
Developing and Maintaining Mental Toughness 89
    Self-Confidence for Mental Toughness.................................. 89
    Coping with Adversity 90
    Practice as you Compete 92
    Pressure Testing... 92
    Consequence Training and Burning-Bridges Training.............. 93
    Mastering Failure... 94
    Exposing Players to Foreign Conditions 95
    Team Building 96
Summary.. 97
Further reading: 98
Advanced reading:... 98

Chapter 6 – Playing Confidently   99

What is Self-Confidence? 100
What is Team Confidence? 102
Where does Confidence come from? 103
The Effects of Confidence on Cricket Performance 107
Enhancing Self- and Team Confidence 109
Imagery 109
Modelling 110
Self-Talk 111
Hypnosis 113
Control the Controllables 114
'Be a good coach to yourself' 115
Body Language 116
Food for Confidence Thoughts 117
Summary 117
Further reading: 118
Advanced reading: 118
Resources 119

Chapter 7 – Controlling Your Emotions   121

What are Emotions? 122
Emotions and Cricket Performance 123
Strategies to Develop Emotional Control 132
Reflection 132
Self-Awareness 133
Cue Words 134
Imagery 135
Music 137
Focused Breathing 138
Summary 139
Further Reading: 140
Advanced reading: 140
Resources 141

Chapter 8 – Leadership and Captaincy   145

What is Leadership? 146
The Effects of Leadership on Cricket 148
The Role of the Cricket Captain 148
Becoming a better Leader and Captain 151
Man-Management 154
Communication 155

Resolving Conflict.. 158
Summary.. 159
Further reading: 160
Advanced reading:... 160

Chapter 9 – Preparing to Perform: Playing to Your Strengths 161
Preparing to Perform 162
What is Preparation?.. 164
The Effects of Preparation on Cricket..................................... 165
Preparing Effectively... 167
Playing to your Strengths 171
What are Strengths?... 172
How does an understanding of strengths affect cricket?......... 173
Summary.. 174
Further reading: 175
Advanced reading:... 175

Chapter 10 – Building a Successful Cricket Team 177
What is a Successful Cricket Team? 179
The Effects of Togetherness on the Team................................ 180
Building a Better Team 188
Summary.. 193
Further reading: 194
Advanced reading:... 194

Chapter 11 – Effective Decision Making 195
What is Decision-Making? 196
The Effects of Decision-Making on Cricket Performance................. 199
Enhancing Decision-Making.. 203
Summary.. 207
Further reading: 208
Advanced reading:... 208

End of Play 209

Start of Play

Anyone who has played, or coached, cricket is aware that the mental side of the game separates the best players from the rest. Indeed, many players, coaches, and commentators describe the substantial contribution psychology plays in determining levels of cricket performance. *The Psychology of Cricket* is the first book to provide sport psychologists, coaches, and players of all levels, with expert knowledge on gaining the mindset necessary to maximize cricket performance.

This book will teach you to apply mental skills effectively in specific practice and match situations, while also getting inside advice from the authors who have experience and expertise of working as sport psychologists in professional cricket.

Through *The Psychology of Cricket*, you'll learn new ways to become mentally tough which include building confidence, improving concentration, enhancing emotional control, staying motivated, and handling pressure. You will also develop your understanding of the important ingredients of successful teams and begin to understand the art of captaincy and effective leadership. Central to this book is the development of the reader's understanding of how psychological factors influence performance, and how knowing this can help to enhance psychological performance.

The Psychology of Cricket starts with an emphasis on individual player development and the fundamental psychological skills you need to excel at the sport. In later chapters, the focus shifts to the importance of team dynamics and mental strategies in competitive play.

For the definitive word on mental preparation, *The Psychology of Cricket* draws on the experiences of sport psychologists, coaches, and players working in cricket at all levels. If you want to gain expert, contemporary advice about developing the correct mindset and mental approach to arguably one of the most psychological sports around, then *The Psychology of Cricket* is the resource for you!

This booked is aimed at cricket players and coaches of all levels across the world. The book will further appeal to parents of young cricketers along with students and practitioners involved in applied sport psychology. Finally, cricket-coaching courses around the world (e.g., Australia, United Kingdom, South Africa, and New Zealand) now integrate psychology components into their delivery. Therefore, this book will also support a learner's understanding of the mental aspects of the game on these courses.

The book initially concentrates on the individual player and the key psychological factors and mental skills that are pertinent to successful cricket performance. There is then a slight shift in focus to look at issues surrounding team dynamics, and leadership.

Each chapter will contain a brief discussion of the main psychological topic by drawing on contemporary theory, research, and experience in a manner that is readable for a wide audience. Following this key mental skills and techniques will be introduced to the reader to enable personal development.

The Psychology of Cricket provides expert advice on key psychological issues and mental skills pertinent to successful cricket performance. The book will also develop the readers' knowledge on applying mental toughness at an individual and team level. In achieving these aims the book offers self-help instructions, throughout, for the development and use of mental skills and techniques.

Stewart Cotterill and Jamie Barker (March 2013)

1

The Mental Side of Cricket

"I think ability is a 10 to 20 per cent requirement, you need 80 to 90 per cent mental strength." Glenn McGrath

"Hard work has to back up ability." Wasim Akram

"Cricket is a game that obviously requires talent, but when talent is equal, as it so often is, the formula for success comes from strength of mind." Steve Waugh

Cricket is an exciting and passionate game. It is a very different game from most other team sports. On the one hand it is a team game played by eleven individuals who combine to form an effective fielding unit, where thinking and acting as one is the ultimate aim (similar to sports such as football, rugby, and basketball). On the other hand cricket is an individual sport with the batsman playing, in some senses, for themselves and their own individual performance.

At the same time cricket is also a contest between two individuals where the batsman and bowler spar and joust to try and get the upper hand in an attempt to land the knockout blow. Due to all of these factors the mental challenges of the game of cricket are very diverse.

The challenges are further compounded by the existence of different formats for the game. Cricket can be played over many days (usually three, four, or five days), over one day (40 or 50 overs), or over just a few hours (in the case of T20 cricket). This further increases the range of challenges facing a successful cricketer. While a game can last for a number of days, it should all, ultimately, come down to the same simple focus, what you do on a ball-by-ball basis. The best players have strategies to ensure that whatever the situation, whatever the score and however they feel, for each delivery they are as prepared as they were for the last ball.

Chapter 1

The biggest challenge to a cricketer is not the learning of the skills (most players have a reasonable, if sometimes flawed, technique), often the biggest challenge is being able to deal with all the factors that can affect your mind and your thinking during a game.

Our experiences of working with professional cricketers tells us that mental factors are often the most important influencers of success and failure. Therefore, this chapter, and the rest of the book, will seek to highlight the main psychological factors that impact upon a player's (and team's) ability to play the game. Subsequent chapters will explore each of these psychological factors in greater detail, and explore strategies that can be used to enhance the player's ability to control and enhance each of these psychological factors.

What is the Mental Game?

Very simply the mental game relates to all of the psychological factors that can impact upon each cricketer's ability to perform. In essence the mental game, and sport psychology in general, is based around common sense principles, which are too often neglected by players. For example, players know that they should remain focused during an innings and believe in their abilities. But the reality is somewhat different to this with players often becoming distracted and doubting their skills.

Feelings and thoughts play a big part in influencing the way that you play in a number of ways.

First, you have to have the *confidence* to be able to execute your skills. There is no point developing a new delivery or shot (such as Kevin Pietersen's switch hit) if you don't have the confidence to use the shot in a game. Also, when you are not feeling confident you don't commit to the shot fully, and as a result do not execute the skills effectively. Supporting this point, the sport psychology research literature demonstrates that self-confidence is one of, if not the most important psychological factors in relation to sport performance.

Second, in our own work, we also find that most cricketers who play at a high level will talk about the importance of the ability to focus. Being 'switched on' when it matters is important. The batsman and bowler need to be focused on the next delivery. There is no point in dwelling on the past or focusing too far in the future. The past is gone (you can think about it after the game) and unless you are successful in the next delivery you might not get to the powerplay, or the next over. So focusing (deliberately thinking about something) is important.

Third, decision-making is also a crucial mental skill for cricketers. How do you decide which shot to play, which delivery to bowl, which field placings to go with? There are important thought processes that underpin all of the decisions that you make, and these thought processes are part of the mental game.

Fourth, we know that when cricketers get too emotional their performance suffers. Being too angry, or frustrated, or stressed will have a negative effect on your game. So, understanding the factors that cause emotions is important. In turn, understanding the triggers for these emotions is an important step in taking control of them. If you understand the emotional triggers you can do something about these emotions and the affect they have on your game. The final aspect of emotions (or strong feelings) is looking at strategies to control and ultimately release them. It would be crazy to try and stop cricketers from experiencing emotions. Cricketers are human, and humans are emotional. But what we can look to do is to develop each cricketer's ability to not get overly emotional, and then to release these emotions, so for the next delivery they are back in their optimal performance state (mindset).

Finally, another important factor influencing the mental game is self-awareness. Good players (at any level) know what their strengths are - essentially knowing what they are good at (and not so good at). As important as this is though, knowing what mental state you need to be able to perform effectively within, is also crucial. If, when playing well, you don't *take time* to understand how and why you are playing well, you will take much longer to recover from poor form. This is because you won't know 'what it is' that you do when you are playing well. In our work we also find that encouraging players to be philosophical and logical about cricket and hence not too obsessive is important in maintaining confidence and emotional stability.

Preparation to play is another important mental aspect of the game of cricket. Effective preparation will enable a greater transfer of performance from training to competition. Practicing for the environment rather than just practicing the skills is central to this. In order to practice how you play you need to be motivated and set yourself effective targets and goals. This is one of the most important ways you can put pressure on yourself to try and replicate what you experience when playing. We regularly encourage players to 'practice as they compete' to ultimately make the demands of practice so high that competition becomes easier or at least players feel more comfortable when going into the stress of competition. It is never going to be exactly the same, but from a psychological perspective it can get pretty close. By not allowing yourself to 'get away' with poor or lazy performances in training you can better prepare for performance.

Coping with setbacks and coping with pressure is another important aspect of the mental game of cricket. In any situation where you want a certain outcome there will be pressure. The more you want it, the more pressure there can be. The mental game also focuses on dealing with this pressure to allow yourself to be able to just execute the skills (just like you would in the nets). In some of our work we find that individuals and teams who struggle in dealing with pressure often practice with low intensity, and no consequences, meaning that when faced with a major final or high-pressure situation they feel less comfortable and underperform.

How Does the Mind Affect Cricket Performance?

Whenever you learn something it gets programmed into the brain. The more you do it the stronger this programming becomes (this works if you are getting it right or if you keep making the same mistakes). These thoughts or behaviours become habits. So, in certain situations you will behave or think in a certain way. Under pressure the way that you think or behave will be driven by your habits. This is the key idea behind learning a skill. If you stand and face a cricket ball being bowled at you once (after being shown the right technique) chances are you will not get it right the next time. After repeating the skill 100 times you are more likely to use the right technique; after 10,000 balls you are far more likely to use the right technique.

There are two important messages here that need to be understood. The first is that practice makes relatively permanent changes (once something becomes a habit it is very difficult to change it), the second is that your brain is always learning what you do, and the way that you did it. So, if you are always told you are not very good - over time you will start believing you are not very good. Then, when it matters, you will *think* you are not good enough. If you always let yourself get angry and frustrated in training, you will probably get angry and frustrated at some point in a game. Players who say they can 'do it differently in a game' are either lying or delusional. What you practice (and therefore what you learn) will ultimately be what you play. Practice hard and play easy!

Another important aspect of the mental game relates to the fact that when you are awake you are thinking. Sometimes you are not aware of it, but nevertheless you are always thinking. Someone who is focused has a specific thing that they are thinking about (hence the term – focused). If you are not focused (e.g., not watching the ball) there is the potential that you will become distracted.

Sometimes, being distracted is simply 'not very useful' (e.g., daydreaming), but at other times it can have a *negative impact* upon performance (such as worrying, having negative thoughts, or not being able to focus on the game). Understanding this challenge, the best players develop strategies that allow them to focus when it matters, by deliberately thinking about certain things to stop other thoughts getting in the way. Surprisingly, many players we have worked with do not have well developed, or clearly defined routines, to allow them to concentrate effectively during cricket. As a result this is an area that sport psychologists and coaches do a lot of work with players on.

Strategies to Become Mentally Stronger

Self-awareness and honesty are core to being mentally stronger and enhancing your mental game. If you don't know what you do, and how you do it, how can you replicate it? This might be fine when you are playing well, but if your form deserts you - how do you get it back? Spending some time to understand what you do and how you do it is important. Also, being honest is crucial. The players who realise their potential will honestly appraise their current expertise and skill levels.

Chapter 1

In doing this they are better placed to improve because they know what to do.

We all want to be the best we can be, but unless you are honest regarding your current levels you will not improve as much as you could. We further encourage players to reflect on their own cricket. In essence, what have they done well and how they can improve. Helping players to recognise, reflect upon, and change unhelpful thoughts (i.e., "I must score runs or I am failure") is a skill which can help them to stay emotionally calmer (i.e., reduce anxiety) but one which will ultimately help their performance.

We find that a lot of players will focus too much on the negative aspects of their game. Too often they will worry about technical flaws or poor performances whilst ignoring the strengths they have. To this end, getting a player to develop 'super-strengths' (areas in their game where they demonstrate potential for excellence; e.g., hitting over the top, or concentrating for long periods of time) encourages players to take a more positive view of how they practice and perform in cricket.

Sometimes it takes another person to help in this process. This could involve talking to another player, talking to the coach, or increasingly in sport talking to a sport psychologist. Sometimes it is just about another person being able to ask the right questions. At other times the right answers, options and advice are needed.

Another important characteristic with humans is their desire to offer someone else 'advice'. Almost everyone will have an opinion, but be aware that just because they have an opinion, it does not necessarily follow that they know what they are talking about. You need to make sure that you trust the information (rather than necessarily the person).

Other players (even very famous ones) know a lot about what they did or currently do. They might have also observed what other people did. You should, however, seek out people who have knowledge as well as experience.

In getting better as a batsman you will spend time with the batting coach. You will talk to other players and ask for their views, but the batting coach understands a range of techniques and how (and importantly why) these techniques are successful. It is the same with the mental game; make sure the people whose advice you seek know 'why' as well as 'how'.

Good coaches understand the mental side of the game and how to develop it. Qualified sport psychologists have an even wider and more comprehensive knowledge base from which to draw when called upon to improve player awareness, mental well-being, and to optimize performance.

Gaining Further Support

In simple terms, the greatest players 'get' the psychology of cricket. The words that they use and the way they view the challenges may be different, but they have developed, over time, a fundamental understanding of the psychological challenges of cricket. For example, Glenn McGrath reportedly used to sing his favourite song to himself whilst standing at the end of his run-up to help him deal with high-pressure situations. More recently, Jonathan Trott has demonstrated a consistent pre-delivery routine that assists him in being able to concentrate for long-periods of time whilst staying calm and composed at the crease.

The development of effective mental skills has sometimes been achieved through working with senior players or experienced coaches, but increasingly this is through talking to, and working with qualified psychological practitioners who understand the psychological challenges of cricket and are able to empower the player to develop their own understanding of the mental side of the game. In the same way that a technical coach will help you develop your skills (technical ability) a mental coach (psychologist) will help you to get better at the mental side of your game and help you to understand and develop a recipe for success.

At this point it is important to draw a distinction between the different types of people who might be able to help. As touched upon above, fellow players can be a good source of ideas and views regarding what it takes to be successful in the mental game. The drawback though is that any player's view is usually (understandably) clouded by what works for them during times of success. There are lots of different types of player with different strengths and weaknesses to their game.

As a result, it makes sense to think that the techniques and strategies that work for one player might not necessarily work for another player. Ask other players what they do, and what works for them, but you need to think about whether this is the best way for you. On the plus side, the things that other players tell you generally have the advantage of being tested in the 'heat of battle'.

A second source of good psychological information can come from the coach. Increasingly the mental game is forming a central component of coach education programmes in cricket across the world. This is making the language that coaches use in talking about the mental side of the game more uniform. That said, good coaches usually have a good understanding of many of the mental challenges facing cricketers; in many cases from both playing and coaching the game. Again, the advantage of talking to the coach, particularly if you work with them a lot, is that they generally know you and your game (which helps them know what might work for you). In turn, their experience is cricket specific so the coach can offer advice regarding what you might try to help your mental game.

The main drawback to using other players and coaches is that often they can tell you about a technique that has worked for someone, but not really tell you *why* it worked. Also, some players will feel uncomfortable disclosing information about mental frailties to their coaches because of possible de-selection. So you might only hear about the times when one particular approach was successful. This is where the psychologist comes in.

The sport psychologist should be able to offer advice and suggest techniques to enhance your mental game, but crucially also be able to explain *how* and *why* they work. This is important because if you understand how and why something works you can modify or enhance it to be most effective for you. So the big advantage that the psychologist has is that they will have a very good knowledge base upon which they can help you build your game and build your awareness as a person - helping you to develop life skills which you can use away from cricket.

Sport psychologists will usually have a good track record in helping other performers as well (I would always recommend finding out how successful they have been in the past). But, there are potentially two main drawbacks to using a psychologist (or mental coach). Firstly (and most obviously) they are experts in psychology. So, if you employ or consult a sport psychologist their expertise is in sport, but it might not necessarily be in cricket. So, working with someone who has experience and expertise in cricket is an important factor. This is mainly for two reasons. First, if they have a track record in the game they will understand the game, how it works, and what the rules are. Being able to concentrate for a whole day in the field is a different type of skill to a soccer player who has a maximum 'game time' of 90 minutes. The second factor relates to the techniques and strategies that they will recommend. If they have worked with cricketers previously then they will have developed techniques that work in cricket, which is also an important consideration.

The other challenge for the sport psychologist relates to the relationships they build with players. They can only really be effective in working with you if they can develop a good working relationship with you. The coach who works with you will often know you as a person, and can modify what they do, and what they say, based upon this knowledge. So for the sport psychologist getting to know the player is also important. To be really effective in developing strategies and techniques - a sport psychologist needs to know how to customize their knowledge and interactions for each individual player.

Regarding the sport psychologist that you work with, you also need to be aware of the qualifications that they have. One thing we have learnt in our years of working in cricket as sport psychologists is that there are plenty of people out there who will offer you advice. Unfortunately a lot of this is unhelpful advice, usually because the people offering the advice don't actually know what they are talking about. Most of this advice will be well meaning, but you need to be able to determine whose advice is valuable, or useful, and whose is not.

With a sport psychologist we find a good test is to ask yourself 'does this person know more than my coach'? If they really are an expert in what they do then the answer to this question should be *yes*. Coaches have a reasonable understanding of the mental game, so if the sport psychologist knows less than the coach, stick with the coach.

True sport psychologists are experts in psychology, and applying it to sport. The sort of experts you should be looking to work with should have trained for a number of years and be professionally qualified. Now, the qualifications change from country to country, but you should expect these professionals to have at least two degrees, and a sport-specific psychology qualification. It is the application of psychology to sport (and cricket in particular) that is important. So, a well-qualified psychologist might not be the right person because while they might be great at psychology they might not be great at applying it to, and working in, sport.

In the United Kingdom (UK) to the use the term 'Sport and Exercise Psychologist', an individual (by legislation) has to be registered with the Health and Care Professions Council (HCPC) as a practicing psychologist. Individuals with these titles are deemed to have sufficient knowledge, skills, and expertise to practice ethically as psychologists.

The professional benchmark for psychologists in the UK is achieving Chartered status with the British Psychological Society (BPS). You can search for qualified sport psychologists in the UK using either the HCPC (http://www.hpc-uk.org) or BPS (http://www.bps.org.uk) consultant finder services. A similar service is available in Australia via the Australian Psychological Society (http://www.psychology.org.au) and in New Zealand via the New Zealand Psychological Society (http://www.psychology.org.nz). If you are looking for a psychologist in India a good starting point is to consult the National Academy of Psychology India (http://www.naopindia.org).

The Benefits of Working with a Sport Psychologist

A sport psychologist can help in a number of ways. These vary from helping you to understand yourself (as a person) better and improving confidence and emotional control, to dealing with significant setbacks and executing your skills most effectively under pressure. As mentioned previously though, how effective the sport psychologist can be is dependent on the relationship that they develop with you. If they do not take the time to get to know and understand you, then chances are they will not be particularly effective in helping you. A key part of the process for the psychologist is to understand you and to understand the challenges that you face, alongside the current state of your mental game. This is usually achieved through three main channels.

First, through the use of conversation. There is no substitute for sitting down with someone and having a chat. Obviously the degree to which you are open and honest will have an impact here.

The second channel is via observation. Sometimes we are not always aware of how we react in certain situations, so the sport psychologist spending some time to watch you play is important. Also, observing you in both practice and competition is important. In practice you could be great at controlling your emotions, but in a game that is where you fall apart. If the sport psychologist doesn't observe the games then there is a chance they might not know this.

Third, sport psychologists often use a range of questionnaires that are designed to find out specific information about you. This information can vary from getting to understand your personality better, to specific detail about your ability to focus, or to explore how mentally tough you are.

Sometimes a sport psychologist is employed to work at a team rather than an individual level. In these situations the way that the sport psychologist works, and what they focus on, might be different. At a team level the sport psychologist will be interested in developing the togetherness (cohesion) of the team, enhancing communication and generally looking to improve how the team works. The sport psychologist can also work with leaders in the team (such as the captain and coach) to maximise their effectiveness and working relationship. The sport psychologist will often work with the coaches to ensure that practice and drills achieve the designed outcomes.

The location in which this help might be provided can also vary. It could be a one-to-one conversation over coffee in a café, or a session with the psychologist at their office, but predominantly, for a sport psychologist, it should be in and around cricket.

Effective sport psychologists recognise that the greatest impact and the greatest learning takes place in the cricket environment. So conversations in and around the nets, or on game days are desirable in most cases. This makes sense for three main reasons. First, you (the player) will feel far more comfortable most of the time in and around cricket. Second, the times when the mental challenges exist will be in and around cricket (practicing or playing); as a result you are far more likely to be able to talk about something when it has just happened (because you remember it). Third, the strategies/skills that you develop to enhance your mental game are far more likely to be effective if they are developed and practiced whilst batting, bowling or fielding. In a similar way to technical skills, you have to practice in the right environment to ensure the greatest transfer into the real game environment. So too with mental skills. They need to be developed, and then practiced in the real environment to be most effective. There are times when the process has an extra step, so you might talk through an issue with the psychologist off the pitch, and then once a strategy is developed look to incorporate this strategy and subsequent techniques into practice and play.

Summary

The game of cricket offers many mental challenges for players and hence sport psychology is now recognised as an integral part of a player's development for optimising performance alongside the establishment of positive mental health.

The key mental aspects affecting individual cricket performance are typically confidence, concentration, and emotions. Therefore sport psychologists can assist players in developing mental skills to develop these areas along with becoming more self-aware, being more equipped to deal with pressure, and becoming a more consistent performer.

In the following chapters we will explore some of the key psychological aspects relating to cricket performance along with outlining skills and suggestions for player development. Ultimately, at the end of this book you should have a better understanding of your game and the areas that you need to develop. More importantly, we also hope you will be armed with mental skills that you can take into your practice and game environments - allowing you to optimise your motivation, confidence, enjoyment, and performance in cricket. We hope you enjoy the journey!

2

Being Motivated and Committed in Cricket

"I have always been motivated and I love this sport. I grew up loving this sport and as each day goes by I fall in love with this game more and more. I am actually proud of the fact that I have been able to play for twenty years and I am still motivated and I want to go out there and do better." Sachin Tendulkar

Cricket is a demanding sport. It requires a considerable amount of time and effort working on the technical, mental (e.g., concentration and confidence), and physical (e.g., balance and strength) aspects of the game. A strong dedication is therefore needed if a cricketer is ever going to master the skills needed to become a top-class player.

However, it can be difficult to put effort into certain aspects of cricket. It can be hard to train. It can be tough to bat in conditions that are unfamiliar or testing. It can be difficult to bowl at two batsmen who have been at the crease for a number of hours and are seemingly immovable. Nevertheless, putting effort into these kinds of tasks is vital if a player is to reach the top of the cricketing world. These examples therefore pose the question *"How do you make sure you are motivated to do everything you need to do to become a good cricketer?"*

The main aim of this chapter is to explore the concept of motivation. Over a series of sections we will define motivation (and the different types of motivation that exist), explore the many ways in which motivation impacts performance, investigate the key determinants of motivation in cricket, and examine a psychological strategy that is proven to enhance and maintain motivation in cricket.

Chapter 2

What is Motivation?

Motivation is the drive that causes you to do something. Whether it is getting out of bed at 6am or going for a 5-mile run on a cold and wet wintery morning we need some kind of motivation behind our actions.

In cricket your motivation for any task can be split into three main components. First, you will decide you want to do something. Next you will put in effort. Finally you will sustain your effort over time (this is called persistence).

Think about any shot you have played or any delivery you have bowled. At some point you would have decided that you wanted to learn how to play this shot or bowl this delivery. As a result you would have put effort into practicing in the nets and you would have consulted your coach for expert technical advice. And after more practice, and more consultation with your coach, there would come a point where you could play this shot or bowl this delivery well on a consistent basis. Motivation is therefore critical if you aspire to perform to your best and reach your potential.

Motivation in cricket can come from different sources. On the one hand motivation can come from inside you (this is known as intrinsic motivation). Intrinsic motivation means that you do something because it is enjoyable and it gives you pleasure. For instance you may work on your technique because you find that developing as a cricketer is enjoyable, satisfying, and gives you a feeling of self-worth.

On the other hand motivation can come from outside you (this is called extrinsic motivation). Extrinsic motivation means that you do something because you will be rewarded or you will avoid a punishment. For example you may work on your technique because becoming a better player will enable you to gain a contract with a team (which is a reward). In another instance you may train hard simply because you do not want to be dropped from your team for being unfit (which is a punishment). Whatever task you are engaged in - your motivation will either be intrinsic, extrinsic, or a combination of both.

Take a moment to think about your own motivation for playing cricket. Is this motivation intrinsic? Is this motivation extrinsic? Is this motivation both intrinsic and extrinsic in nature? Being aware of your motivation for a task is important because both intrinsic and extrinsic motivation will have an impact on your performance.

The Effects of Motivation on Cricket Performance

"Only I know whether I am motivated enough or passionate enough to be part of the game. I kept telling myself I need to enjoy the game. If I am not enjoying the challenges associated with the game, then it does not work." Sachin Tendulkar

Research in sport tells us that intrinsic motivation is good for your performance (see Figure 2.1). The main reason why intrinsic motivation is good for your performance is related to effort. When you find something interesting and enjoyable (such as opening the batting or bowling) you will invest a considerable amount of effort into it. And the more effort you put into something the more you will reach your potential in that task.

To help you understand the link between interest and effort imagine you are about to start washing-up some pots. If you enjoy washing-up (which may be rare) you will put all your effort into making sure the pots are as clean as possible. If you do not enjoy washing-up (which may be more common) you will put less effort into ensuring that the pots are clean (and as a result the pots will probably need washing again). Putting effort into something is important as you will feel happy, satisfied, and proud of your achievement.

Putting effort into something is also important as you will feel confident. This is because effort increases the likelihood that you will perform well. And when you perform well in cricket you will be confident about repeating a good performance in the future (see *Chapter Six* on *Playing Confidently*). A situation in cricket where effort is particularly important is when you play against an opponent who is as equally talented as you are. The cricketer who succeeds cannot be the one who is the most talented (because both players have the same amount of talent). The cricketer who will come out on top will be the player who puts in the most effort and sticks at their performance.

Another reason why intrinsic motivation is good for your performance is related to concentration. When you are interested you pay attention. A good example might be when you buy a new computer game. Because you enjoy the computer game you spend hours and hours of time playing nothing but the game in an attempt to complete it. You stay in the moment and ignore distractions because you do not want to miss any important information that could be used to complete the game. Overall then, being intrinsically motivated will make you an energetic, confident, and attentive player.

In contrast research in sport tells us that extrinsic motivation is not as good for your performance (see Figure 2.1). The principal reason why extrinsic motivation can hinder your performance is once again linked to concentration (see *Chapter Three* on *Staying Focused*).

When you do something to gain a reward or to avoid a punishment you will focus on an outcome. Imagine that your outcome is to keep your place in your team. Focusing on this outcome will become a distraction. This is because you will pay attention to information that is irrelevant to your cricketing performance. For example you may pay attention to internal thoughts about what it would mean to keep your place in your team, or what the consequences would be if you do not retain your place. As a result you will not attend to information that is relevant to your cricketing performance (such as watching the ball as a batsman, or bowling a consistent line and length as a bowler). Thinking too much about the future and not staying in the moment will be detrimental to your performance because you will ignore the things you need to do to achieve your outcome.

A second reason why extrinsic motivation can hinder your performance is associated with anxiety. This is because any outcome in cricket (e.g., winning a game) depends on a number of factors. Some of these factors you have control over (such as your own performance) and other factors you have no control over (such as the opposition or the pitch conditions). Thinking about things you cannot control will make you anxious.

Additionally, because the outcome of any event in cricket is in the future - you will start to ponder about what you think *should* and *must* happen. Someone focusing on an outcome is likely to think along the lines of "*I must achieve my outcome to be a good player*" or "*If I do fail to achieve my outcome then this means I am a bad cricketer*". And in an instance when you do not achieve your outcome this can make you even more stressed and anxious.

A good example of this mindset is playing the board game 'Monopoly'. The main objective of Monopoly is to make your way around a board and buy properties. Each time an opponent lands on a property you own they pay you rent. To win a game of Monopoly you must make all other players bankrupt. If you focus on the outcome of Monopoly (making people bankrupt) you will concentrate on buying the most properties on the board or the properties that charge the highest rent. And when an opponent has more properties than you, or owns the properties that charge the most rent, you will become frustrated, lose interest, and want to start a new game. This is different to someone who enjoys playing Monopoly. They will play the game to its conclusion regardless of whether they have the most properties or the properties that charge the highest rent. In turn they will feel calm and composed. Overall then, being extrinsically motivated will cause you to become distracted and make you a frustrated, anxious, and potentially fragile cricketer.

Figure 2.1, The effect of intrinsic and extrinsic motivation on cricket performance.

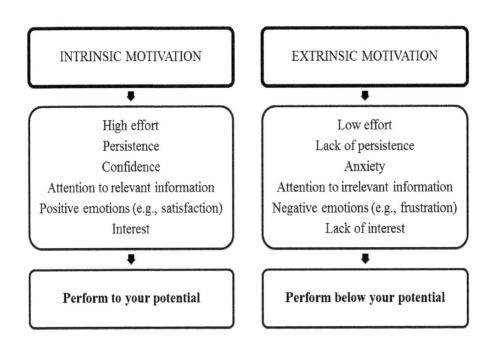

Outlook and its Influence on Cricket Motivation

The way in which you define achievement in cricket will influence your motivation. On one hand you can interpret achievement to mean that you have improved in an area of your game or mastered a specific skill. This is known as a task-oriented mindset (see Figure 2.2).

Being a task-oriented cricketer will cause you to be motivated to succeed in all aspects of your game in order to become a better player. This means that anything you achieve in cricket will be compared against your own personal standards (or self-referenced) and not compared against the standards of any other player.

The fact that achievement is self-referenced is the main reason that a task-oriented mindset is related to intrinsic motivation. Also, because a task-oriented cricketer will perceive achievement to mean that they are competent, they will experience feelings of enjoyment, satisfaction, and self-worth (which are all features of intrinsic motivation). A task-oriented mindset is therefore good for your performance. This is because focusing on personal improvement will require you to pay attention to the right information, channel your effort into a task, and persist for the entire duration of the task (without any of these things you will not be able to improve). It follows that when you improve, or master a task, you will gain confidence from becoming competent at being able to do that task successfully.

On the other hand you can interpret achievement to mean that you are superior to other players. This is termed an ego-oriented mindset (see Figure 2.2). Being an ego-oriented cricketer will cause you to be motivated to succeed in all aspects of your game in order to demonstrate that you are the better player. This means that anything you achieve will be compared against other players' personal standards (or other-person referenced) rather than compared against your own personal standards.

Another feature of this ego-oriented mindset is that in moments where your achievement matches that of another player you will believe that your achievement required considerably less effort. Given that achievement is referenced to other people, an ego-oriented mindset is related to extrinsic motivation. And just like extrinsic motivation, research tells us that an ego-oriented mindset can hinder your performance. This is mainly because having an ego-oriented mindset will cause you to focus on the performance of others (which is something that you have *no control* over and is a distraction) rather than focusing on your own performance (which are the things you *can control* like effort and persistence).

Remember, trying to control an uncontrollable will make you anxious. The main problem arises when you have an ego-oriented mindset and you fail to demonstrate superior performance. You will interpret this to mean you are incompetent which will cause you to withdraw effort, give up easily, and feel dejected and unconfident that you can achieve success in the future.

The mindset you adopt as a cricketer will be heavily influenced by the people around you (such as coaches, teammates, support staff, family, and peers). The way in which these people speak to you and behave towards you will create an environment. This environment is known as a motivational climate.

In cricket, two motivational climates exist. The first is called a task-oriented climate which emphasizes the importance of getting better as a player and as a result will motivate you to adopt a task-oriented mindset. An individual in your own cricket network will support a task-oriented climate when they ask you a question concerning your own skill development (e.g., *"Have you improved recently?"* or *"Do you feel you are making progress?"*) and will reinforce a task-oriented climate when they provide you with feedback on your performance (e.g., *"You need to keep your head still when playing a shot"* or *"You need to raise your bowling arm higher"*) and reward improvement.

The second type of motivational climate that other people can create is called an ego-oriented climate. This climate stresses the importance of being the better player and as a result will motivate you to adopt an ego-oriented mindset. Someone in your cricket network will support an ego-oriented climate when they ask a question regarding an outcome (e.g., *"Did you beat them today?"* or *"Were you the best player on your team?"*) and will reinforce an ego-oriented climate when they provide you with feedback on your results (e.g., *"You won"* or *"You lost"*) and reward superior performance.

Interestingly, players coached in an ego-orientated climate are more likely to adopt a *win at all costs* mentality and engage in unsportsmanlike behaviours. Ultimately, be aware that your mindset can be shaped by other people and each of these mindsets carries a certain set of consequences (see Figure 2.2).

Figure 2.2, The effects of task-oriented and ego-oriented mindsets on cricket performance.

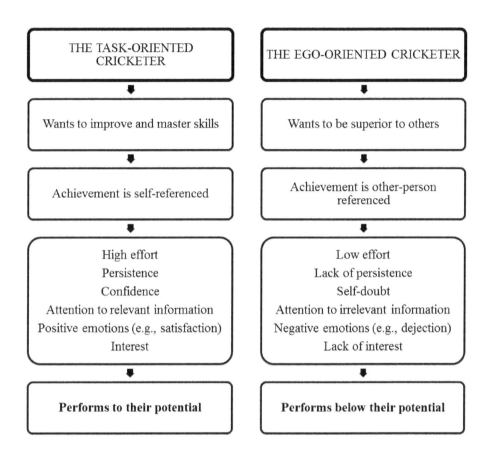

Factors Influencing Cricket Motivation

There are a number of other factors that will influence your motivation in cricket (see Figure 2.3). The first is related to confidence. We know from our work that a confident cricketer is a motivated cricketer. This is because confident cricketers believe that succeeding at a task (such as batting through an innings or claiming the wickets of top order batsmen) is possible. And when you believe that you can achieve something you will try hard, and keep going, until you have succeeded.

On the other hand we know that a cricketer who is short on confidence will also be low in motivation. This is because unconfident cricketers doubt their ability to succeed at a task. And when you have sufficient self-doubt you will not try hard and will withdraw effort when faced with a difficult situation (e.g., a wicket that is tough to bat on).

The second factor that can impact upon your motivation is related to anxiety. As cricketers you can perceive symptoms of anxiety (e.g., butterflies in the stomach or sweaty palms) to be good or bad. When you perceive these symptoms to be good you will say things like "*I am ready*" or "*This is my moment*" These kinds of statements mean that you will *want to approach a situation* and as a result you will display a series of helpful behaviours. These behaviours are called approach behaviours. Some good examples of approach behaviour include:

- Careful planning (e.g., thinking about field placements that will limit the opportunities of a batsman to score runs)
- Problem-solving (e.g., trying to figure out the best way to bat or bowl on a wicket)
- Taking ownership (e.g., attempting to keep the strike or asking to bowl the next over)

However, when you perceive the anxiety you experience to be bad you will say things like "*I do not want to do this*" or "*This is awful*". Thinking this way means that you will want to avoid or run away from a situation and as a result you will display a series of unhelpful behaviours. These behaviours are called avoidance behaviours. Classic avoidance behaviours include:

- Speeding-up the execution of a skill (e.g., rushing through a shot or a delivery)
- Procrastination (e.g., "*I'll bowl later*" or "*Give me a few more minutes to put my pads on*")
- Nervous habits (e.g., biting your nails or fidgeting)
- Trying to escape a situation (e.g., by feigning an injury and leaving the field)

An avoidance behaviour is therefore a deliberate attempt to disengage with a situation which will result in a lack of motivation.

The third factor that can influence your motivation is related to emotions. It is likely that you will experience a loss of form or be dropped from your team at some point in your career. Your immediate response to poor performance will always be emotional in nature. That is completely normal (see the *Chapter* on *Controlling Your Emotions*). For example you may begin to think things such as "*I am simply not good enough*" or "*Other cricketers are better than me*". It is important to recognize that you are more likely to throw in the towel when you act upon such emotionally charged thoughts and feelings. As a result you can expect to struggle to rediscover good performance or your position in your team.

Remember, when you feel incompetent at something you are more likely to be demotivated. In such instances it is vital that you allow yourself time to think. When you give yourself time to think you will begin to see things more logically.

So, after your emotions have cleared you may start to think "*Okay, I just need to keep working hard and I will regain my position in the team*" or "*If I keep trying, the good performances will return*". This mode of thinking will give you the best chance of playing well again or regaining your place in the team.

Remember, when you are motivated you try hard and when you try hard you perform to your potential. West Indian all-rounder Marlon Samuels is a good advocate of using setbacks as a means of motivation. Recently Samuels was quoted as saying "*I use every disappointment to build me as a person. I use all of them to motivate me and I know that if I can overcome all the obstacles put in front of me I can get to where I want to go.*"

Being able to appreciate that setbacks in performance provide an opportunity to reflect, learn, and move forward as a player will be crucial to maintaining your motivation.

Your motivation will also be affected by how important you perceive a task to be. In short when you perceive something as important or meaningful (such as practice) you will choose to do it. You do not need to rely on anyone (e.g., a coach) or anything else (e.g., money) to motivate you. Similar to the Nike motto you "*Just Do It*".

The flipside is that when you fail to see the relevance in something you will often need other people or things to motivate you. A good exercise is to think about an aspect of your game that you struggle to see as important. Do you need encouragement from a coach or teammate to complete this task? Do you need incentives or rewards? If you do, then this is okay *most* of the time. The problem arises when you rely completely on other people or other things for motivation.

As an example, consider the case of Steve. Steve is a cricketer who does not think fitness is important for his cricket. To be motivated to complete fitness sessions Steve has to draw upon the encouragement and praise provided by his fitness coach. However, a few months later Steve's fitness coach is sacked and not replaced. Steve can no longer draw upon encouragement or praise. Now Steve has no motivation at all to work on his fitness. Ultimately Steve has been controlled entirely by an external source of motivation (the fitness coach). Situations like this are unhelpful; when the external source of motivation is withdrawn you will have no drive inside you to fall back on to complete your task.

Other people (such as coaches and teammates) will also affect your motivation in another way. This is related to self-esteem. When you hear comments such as *"We need you because you are an excellent bowler"* or *"Without you we will struggle to score runs"* you will feel wanted. The actions of other people will also make you feel wanted (such as receiving a pat on the back from your coach).

Alastair Cook is a good example of someone who makes his teammates feel wanted. Recently, Cook commented on how much England needed Kevin Pietersen during a one-day series in India. Cook said *"That 100 in Mumbai was such an important innings that proved his worth. Hopefully his experience in these conditions, with the Indian Premier League as well, is something we can use."*

Being made aware that you contribute something (in Pietersen's case experience and runs) will make you feel good about yourself. And being made to feel wanted will motivate you. This is because feeling as though you have worth builds your confidence, makes you feel positive, and most of all tells you that you are good enough to be involved. It follows that anything that suggests you are unwanted or not the right person for a task will harm your motivation. An example of this is when you receive criticism from a coach or teammate (e.g., *"Someone else would have scored more runs"* or *"You should not have bowled today"*).

Feeling that you do not contribute to a task will lower your confidence, make you feel negative, and suggest you are not good enough to be involved. And we know that feeling unwanted will demotivate you. The important point to remember is that words and actions can have a huge impact on your own and others motivation.

A useful exercise to complete is to write down all the things you would want your coach to say to you. Once you have compiled your list go through each point and think whether you say these things to your teammates. Being a good coach to your teammates will make them feel better and motivate them allowing you and your team to reach their potential (also see *Chapter Six* on *Playing Confidently*).

Enhancing Cricket Motivation

"It is important for you to find your mountain or that clear goal as it will give you a sense of purpose and you will put in the required sacrifice." Rahul Dravid

Goal setting is one of the fundamental techniques you should use to motivate yourself as a cricketer. Goals are the things that you try to achieve and are the main objective of anything that you do in cricket.

The first big advantage of having goals is that they will direct your attention towards a specific task. Being able to attend to the right information is critical if you are going to perform to your best. The second real advantage of goal setting is that it will regulate your effort. As we have already explored, effort is important because it allows you to perform to your potential. Goals are also effective because they will cause you to persist until your goal is reached. A final benefit of setting goals as a cricketer is that they will motivate you to find alternative strategies in order to make your goals happen. Problem-solving is particularly important when you are faced with difficulties in your own cricket (such as poor performance) and you need to find a solution.

All cricketers have goals they want to achieve but very few players feel as though their goals are effective. One reason for this is that cricketers commonly set goals that have no direction or lack a clear purpose and as a result their effort is not channelled into a specific task. These goals are known as 'do your best goals' (such as *"My goal is to go out there and give it my all!*"). With this in mind it follows that you need to be aware of the various types of goals you should set yourself to maximise your own motivation.

The first type of goal you should set is an outcome goal that refers to an end result (e.g., "*My goal is to win a game of cricket*"). Having an outcome goal is important because outcome goals motivate you to strive for something in the future. When you have something to aim for as a cricketer you will be committed to achieving that outcome.

However, *only* having outcome goals in cricket will harm your motivation. This is mainly because any outcome in cricket (e.g., winning a game) depends on a number of factors. As we have already explored, some of these factors you have control over (e.g., your own performance) and other factors you have no control over (e.g., the opposition or the conditions). Thinking about things you cannot control will make you anxious and short on confidence. Remember that cricketers who concentrate purely on an outcome will get frustrated, give up, and lose focus on what they need to do to achieve their outcome.

The second type of goal you should set is a performance goal that relates to a specific standard of performance you want to achieve (e.g., "*My goal is to score a century*" or "*My goal is to take 5 wickets*").

Setting yourself a performance goal will be helpful because performance goals motivate you to master a performance. In turn you can check your progress towards achieving your desired outcome.

It is crucial to be aware that *only* setting performance goals in cricket will have a negative effect on your motivation. When you focus entirely on performance you do not concentrate on what it is that you need to do to perform well. This will undermine your interest in cricket. If you have ever viewed a performance as an anti-climax, take a moment to reflect and think "*Was I only concerned about achieving a certain standard of performance?*"

The third and final type of goal you should set therefore is a process goal that relates to your strategy for performing well. A process goal for a batsman may be to "*Use footwork and watch the ball*". A process goal for a bowler could be to "*Run in hard and hit the deck*". Having a process goal in cricket is beneficial because process goals motivate you to concentrate on the things you need to do to achieve your outcome and perform well. Process goals will further motivate you because how you perform as a cricketer is something that you *can control*. Focusing on things that you can control will give you confidence and allow you to stay calm and relaxed.

A process goal can help you feel satisfied and remain interested in your cricket because you will have done everything you could to perform to your best. However, it is important to understand that a process goal can lack purpose if the process (such as the above "*Use footwork and watch the ball*" or "*Run in hard and hit the deck*") is not directed towards an outcome or a standard of a performance.

The key message is that for goal setting to be effective at motivating you as a cricketer - you must set a combination of outcome, performance, and process goals (see Resource 2.1 at the end of this chapter to help you set an appropriate combination of goals in cricket).

Any outcome, performance, or process goals that you set yourself will either relate to your long-term or short-term cricket career. A long-term goal refers to something that you try to achieve in the distant future. An example of a long-term performance goal would be to become the highest run scorer, or wicket-taker, in the history of your team.

On the other hand a short-term goal is a something that you attempt to accomplish in the more immediate future. An example of a short-term performance goal would be to score runs or to take wickets in your next match.

Any long-term goal you set will help your motivation because long-term goals will focus your mind on a daily, weekly, and yearly basis. However, it will be difficult for you to check how you are progressing towards your long-term goal. Short-term goals are therefore crucial because they allow you to measure your progress and readjust your goals if needed.

By achieving your short-term goals you will grow in confidence, remain interested, and stay committed to your long-term goals. To this end, for goal setting to be effective you must set a combination of outcome, performance, and process goals that relate to both your short-term and long-term cricket career.

Now you are aware of the different types of goals you should set you need to be aware of how to set them (using the SMART method). The first step to setting effective outcome, performance, and process goals in both the short and long-term is to make them *specific*.

A specific goal is precise and clear rather than broad and vague. An example of a specific process goal in cricket would be to *"Get to the pitch of the ball"* or to *"Bowl a good line and length"*. Specific goals will motivate you because they help focus your mind by being explicit about what it is you need to do or should try to accomplish. Making sure your goals are specific will also help you measure your progress because you can easily track the behaviours that relate to your goal. In our examples of specific process goals, this would be how often you get to the pitch of the ball, or how many times you bowl a good line and length.

The second step to setting effective goals is to make them *measurable*. A measurable goal can be assessed and will help motivate you because they enable you to check your progress and think about what you should continue, stop, or start doing to attain your goal. These check-points give you a valuable opportunity to receive feedback which will allow you to gain recognition for your effort and receive encouragement that will boost your confidence and interest.

The next stage to setting effective goals is to make them *adjustable*. Adjustable goals are flexible and can be changed. An adjustable goal will keep you motivated at times when you experience a setback in your cricket (such as an injury). This is because a setback can hinder your progress and make your goal too difficult to achieve. Remember, when you perceive that you cannot do something you will lack confidence, become anxious, and eventually withdraw effort.

Adjustable goals are also important when you make progress at a faster rate than you expect. This is because progressing beyond your expectations causes your goal to become easier. The easier your goal becomes the less effort you will expend which will result in you feeling less satisfaction with your achievement (because with *more effort* you could have *achieved more*).

The fourth step to effective goal setting is to set *realistic* goals. A realistic goal is a goal that you are able to do. Realistic goals will motivate you because when you believe something is possible you will put in effort. Be mindful that realistic goals should challenge you (as long as you have the ability to meet your challenge). This is because you will increase your effort when you increase the difficulty of your goal (be conscious that you do not make your goal too difficult as this can lead to frustration). Knowing that you have put everything into accomplishing a challenge will make you feel proud and satisfied with your achievement.

The final stage to effective goal setting is to make sure your goals are *timetabled*. Timetabled goals have a specific time frame in which achievement should occur. A good example of a timetabled outcome goal is to *"Win three 4-day matches in two months"*.

It is important to spend some time thinking about the consequences of the timetable that you set yourself. On one hand a time frame that is unrealistic and too difficult (e.g., *"I want to score a century in 30 balls"* or *"I want to take 4 wickets in an over"*) will result in a series of negative emotions primarily because you will be unlikely to have the competence to achieve your goal. On the other hand a time frame that does not challenge you and is too easy (e.g., *"I want to average 10 runs with the bat this season"* or *"I want to take 5 wickets this season"*) will cause you to feel deflated after your achievement because an easy goal requires minimal effort.

Overall then it is important that the outcome, performance, and process goals you set yourself in the short-term and long-term are:

- Specific
- Measurable
- Adjustable
- Realistic
- Timetabled

Put simply you need to think SMART and be SMART about the goals you set (see Resource 2.2 at the end of this chapter to help you set SMART goals in cricket).

Chapter 2

After you have used the SMART principles to create your goals you should write yourself a contract. This contract should include all the things you need to do in order to achieve your goals (see Resource 2.3 at the end of this chapter to help you develop your contract). For example you may feel that to achieve your goals you need to train hard, make sacrifices (such as limiting your alcohol intake), listen to advice (from coaches and teammates), and practice your technique. Recognizing that you need to behave in a certain way to reach your goals is important as this gives your mind a clear focus on how you will make your goals happen.

In order to make your SMART goals happen you will also need to show a significant amount of commitment. Goal commitment refers to your determination to reach your goals.

There are two main factors that will influence your goal commitment. The first is how important you feel your goals are. The reason for this is that we know you will be interested in doing something that you find important. To make your goals important it is crucial that you take complete authority and assign yourself goals (or at least participate in assigning them) rather than allowing someone else to assign them for you. This is because you own the goals (or partly own them if you have developed them with someone else). Accordingly you should emphasise the importance of your goals by making your goals public. Writing down your SMART goals and placing them somewhere you and others will see them (such as on your fridge and in your changing room) will remind you on a regular basis what you want to achieve (you should also place your contract in the same places). As a matter of your integrity you will feel an obligation to stick to your goals (and your contract) when you disclose them in a public place (see Resource 2.4 at the end of this chapter to help you think of where you can place your SMART goals and contract).

The second factor that will affect how committed you will be to your goals relates to confidence. This is because *believing* that you can attain your goals will cause you to put in effort and persist. Without effort and persistence you cannot perform well. The SMART method of goal setting should make you confident in goal attainment because you will develop goals that are realistic and not too difficult. However making sure you take the time to congratulate and praise yourself for any progress towards your goals will also make you confident that you can achieve them. Take credit for the progress you make because feeling competent will make you believe you can be competent again in the future.

In cricket anything that you are competent and good at is termed a strength. It is important you realize that goal setting can be used to develop your strengths (into super-strengths) just as it can be used to improve your weaknesses (into strengths). To discover your strengths, spend some time thinking about what you are good at in cricket. This could be bowling to left-handed batsmen (like England spin-bowler Graeme Swann) or maintaining concentration for a prolonged period at the crease (like England opening batsman Alastair Cook). Turning your strengths into super-strengths is important because super-strengths will enable you to reach a higher potential that will take your game to a whole new level.

Summary

A recurring theme throughout this chapter has been the importance of motivation in allowing you to perform to your potential. But remember that motivation to engage in cricket-related activities can come from different places (inside and outside of you) and each of these sources of motivation will carry a specific set of consequences.

Since intrinsic motivation is considered to be good for your performance you should try and discover what it is about cricket that you love and focus on this throughout your career. This will help you to perceive cricket as a hobby rather than a chore which is important because tasks that seem like chores are difficult to complete. To ensure that you stick at tasks in cricket and see them out until their completion be sure to set yourself your own targets to chase down.

Key messages:

- Motivation is the drive that causes you to engage in cricket-related activities
- Your motivation will be intrinsic (an inner drive) and/or extrinsic (an outer drive)
- Intrinsic motivation is good for performance

- Extrinsic motivation is not as good for performance (especially complete extrinsic motivation)
- Motivation is affected by your mindset, psychological factors, and other people
- Setting a combination of SMART outcome, performance, and process goals (in both the short and long-term) will enhance and prolong your motivation

Further reading:

Syed, M. (2010). *Bounce: The myth of talent and the power of practice.* Fourth Estate: London.

Advanced reading:

Locke, E. A., & Latham, G. P. (1985). The application of goal setting to sports. *Journal of Sport Psychology*, 7(3), 205-222.

Roberts, G. C., Treasure, D. C., & Conroy, D. E. (2007). Understanding the dynamics of motivation in sport and physical activity. In G. Tenenbaum & R. C. Eklund (Eds.), *Handbook of Sport Psychology* (3rd ed., pp. 3-30). Hoboken, NJ: John Wiley & Sons.

Ryan, R. M., & Deci, E. L. (2000). Self-determination theory and the facilitation of intrinsic motivation, social development, and well-being. *American Psychologist.* 55(1), 68-78.

Goal Setting Resources

Resource 2.1, Setting outcome, performance, and process goals.

At the start of any task you perform in cricket, assign yourself a combination of outcome, performance, and process goals. Make sure you develop each goal in line with the SMART method of goal-setting (see Resource 2.2: Setting SMART goals for guidance). Use the following as a template.

> MY TASK IS...
>
> To just run in and bowl

> MY OUTCOME GOAL IS...
>
> To get the batsman playing forward

> MY PERFORMANCE GOAL IS...
>
> To bowl a full length

> MY PROCESS GOAL IS...
>
> To think that I'm going to get the batsman out every time I bowl a delivery.

Chapter 2

Resource 2.2, Setting SMART goals.

For each outcome, performance, and process goal you set yourself in cricket use the following checklist to make sure your goals are SMART and effective.

Specific: *"Is my goal precise and clear?"*

Measurable: *"Does my goal allow me to check my progress?"*

Adjustable: *"Can I change my goal if it becomes too easy or too difficult?"*

Realistic: *"Does my goal challenge me?"*

Timetabled: *"Does my goal have a time-frame?"*

Resource 2.3, Making goals happen.

To make your goals happen write down the things that you will do to help you achieve your goals.

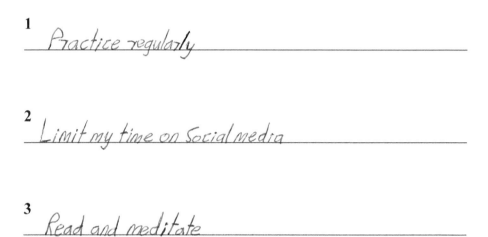

1
Practice regularly

2
Limit my time on Social media

3
Read and meditate

Chapter 2

Resource 2.4, Making goals feel important.

To make your goals feel important list all the places where you will put your goals and your contract so they can be seen by you and others on a daily basis.

1

My room

2

3

3

Staying Focused

"The key to concentration is filling your mind with what you need to do to ensure a successful action, for me to bat there must be nothing but the ball in my mind, this occupies my thoughts before every shot."
Justin Langer

"My best moments as a batsman came when I had no extraneous thoughts in my head. It was about having a clear focus, concentrating wholly on the next ball and playing the best I could." Steve Waugh

In many respects cricket is a simple game. For the batsman the job is to hit the ball. For the bowler the aim is to beat the batsman and take a wicket.

The first challenge for any aspiring cricketer in a quest to achieve these two main aims is to master the required technical skills. This in itself takes many hundreds of hours of practice to form the right habits of skill execution. Without a good, effective, and consistent technique the batsman can't expect to be able to consistently hit the ball. For the bowler, without good control and the ability to vary the types of delivery they bowl, they can't begin to consistently beat the batsman.

However, once these technical skills have been mastered to a reasonable level, further challenges emerge for the cricketer to master. Due to its relatively technical nature, when you are learning to play cricket, your mind is almost completely swamped with technical information and pointers to execute the skill correctly. All of this thinking takes mental effort, which is why learning a new skill is so mentally tiring. But once you move beyond this 'novice' point and start to become a more competent technician, playing the shots and bowling the balls becomes more automatic. This shift to a more 'automatic' execution of the skill works like a reflex, you don't have to think about it, and as such it becomes less mentally draining. However, the issue then arises, what do you focus on?

Chapter 3

The mind is a wonderful thing. A very effective machine, but when we are awake (and often when we are not) it is switched on. When the mind is switched on (just like a car engine) it is always ticking over. This means we are always thinking about something. We might not always be aware of what it is, or remember exactly what it was, but we are always thinking of something. So, returning to the example of learning a skill, we only have a limited capacity for how much we can think about at any one time. This means that when we are thinking about how to execute the new skills we are learning we have no time to think about other things.

But when the skill becomes automatic this 'thinking space' still needs to be filled with something. The question then is what do we fill this space with? If we don't deliberately think of something to fill this space with, there is the potential for anything to pop in there. This is what happens when you are sat listening to someone and your mind wanders and you start daydreaming, or a loud noise grabs your attention, or you are still thinking about the last delivery that you missed. With this last example, if you can only think about one thing at a time, and you are thinking about the last delivery, you are not really focusing on the next delivery (which in cricket is always the most important one). As a result, understanding what it takes to be focused, how to stop being distracted, and understanding what techniques you can use to get better at focusing are crucial.

What is Focusing?

Focusing in sport refers to what you are thinking about (whether deliberately or not). The name comes from the idea of focusing (zooming in on) a particular thing. Focusing is forcing your mind to pay attention to a specific thing at a specific time. If it is *not* a deliberate act then it is *not* seen as focusing.

Often the terms 'concentration' and 'attention' are used to refer to the same thing in cricket. The thing you are focusing on can be external (in the world around you, such as the bowler, a fielder, or the ball), or alternatively it could be internal (your own thoughts, like day dreaming, or doing arithmetic in your head). This focus can also be wide (taking in all the things you can see, such as fielders, the bowler, the spectators and the vista), or very narrow (just focusing on the ball).

The important thing to remember here is that while you 'see' everything, you can only really focus on some of the things that your eyes can see at any one moment in time. A good example to illustrate this would be to turn on the television and sit down and watch the cricket. You can see everything in front of you (the TV, the pictures on the wall, the TV cabinet, the window), but once you start watching the cricket on the TV you are not aware of the pictures on the wall and the TV cabinet. You can 'see' them, but are not focusing on them because you are focusing on the cricket on the TV.

When you start thinking about the pictures on the wall you become less aware of the action on the TV and the game of cricket. This also illustrates another point. Having a limited amount that you can focus on means that the degree of detail you see is also limited. When you pay attention to a broad picture (the fielders) your picture is less detailed regarding each player. To get the degree of detail that you need to focus on the ball when the bowler is running, you need to have a very narrow focus (you can't really 'see' anything else). The implication here is that if you adopt a narrow focus too early you might miss important information about fielders and field positions when batting. But if you focus on the ball it is very difficult for other things to distract you.

The other thing about focusing is that it takes effort and energy. The longer you focus for, the more tiring it is. So, in a game of cricket, trying to focus for the whole game is pretty much impossible. Even in twenty20 games it is not really possible, so playing in three, four, or five-day games focusing for every second of every minute of every hour of the game is just not an option. In international cricket there are drinks breaks within sessions, which help, but even then it is difficult to focus for that long.

Also, the more narrow the focus that you adopt - the more effort it ultimately takes for any given period of time. Adopting a 'wider lens' focus is less tiring both mentally and physically (on the muscles of the eyes). If you ever feel your eyes feeling strained, adopt a wider focus, and try looking at things a long distance away; you will find that your eyes feel less strained and you recover a little mentally.

Just to put into perspective how much effort and energy thinking takes, evidence in neuroscience suggests that the brain 'burns' 25% of all the calories you consume on any given day. No wonder you feel tired after making your brain work hard. So, if you can't focus all of the time, but recognise that you need to focus at specific times, what do you do?

Well the answer is to learn to switch on (focus) and switch off (relax). This is all relative though, so when you switch off you are still in the game, just not focusing as fully as when it is time for the next delivery.

The Effects of Focusing on Cricket

There are a couple of main ways that your ability to focus impacts on your cricket. The first of which is not really related to focusing, it is more about a lack of it. The opposite of being focused is being distracted. This is where something grabs your attention and you stop focusing on what you wanted to, or should be focusing on. Now these distractions can (just like focusing) be either external or internal. External distractions are usually things you hear or things you see. When getting ready to face the next delivery - a couple of words from the wicket keeper, or a shout from the crowd could grab your focus (moving it away from watching the ball). One of the biggest external factors that can distract you, or grab your attention, is when someone says your name. If you think about a time you have been in a crowded room and someone close by says your name in a conversation, you instinctively 'tune in' to that conversation at the expense of what you were previously doing.

Probably more important than external distractions though are the internal distractions that might exist. In this sense we are our own worst enemies. We distract ourselves far more than external distractions do. We do this through the internal 'chat' that takes place in our heads. A good example of this is when you are listening to someone else speak. It is very rare that we actually just listen to the other person speak all the time. Often we listen to parts of what they are saying while also thinking about what we are going to say next. But as soon as we starting thinking about what to say next we are not really listening to what is being said. As a result it is possible to end up having two separate conversations.

This 'thinking of something else when you should be focused' happens in cricket as well. When you should be focusing on the next delivery (batting, bowling, or fielding), you potentially start thinking about something else (which means you are not really focused on the next ball). These distractions can be linked to the game such as thinking *"Okay, I just need to see out the next five overs before lunch"*, or can be linked to something else outside of the game *"How am I going to tell my parents I can't make that dinner they have organised"*.

Often in cricket these distractions relate to dwelling on past events such as thinking *"I can't believe I played that shot"* or thinking about the future, such as *"In the next over I need to ..."* all of which distracts you from the important thing which is focusing on the present (the next ball).

The second important way that focusing affects your cricket is due to the fact that it takes *effort* (as you focus for longer you become more tired). If you stay focused for a long period of time you will become very drained, and unable to think particularly well (make the wrong decisions and play the wrong shots). As a result, effective cricketers need to have a strategy to focus, then focus less intensely, before refocusing (sometimes referred to as switching on and switching off). Otherwise, you will start off playing well but as you become more tired your performance will suffer until you ultimately do something stupid, or execute your skills poorly (dropping catches, bowling in the wrong areas, playing the wrong shots, or just not executing your skills particularly well).

The other way in which focusing affects your performance relates to when you get stressed. As you start to feel the pressure, and become stressed, there is a tendency to try and focus on the mechanics of executing your skills (because you think it is the right thing to do). This is often referred to as 'paralysis by analysis'.

Once a skill has become learnt (and you don't have to think about it) trying to think about the execution of the skill actually makes performance worse (hence the paralysis part) because thinking about it stops you doing the skill fluently (the analysis part).

Also, when you get emotional (usually getting angry or frustrated) it becomes far more difficult to focus and not be distracted. This also links into another aspect of focus - the limited capacity you have to focus with. All tasks require a certain amount of this mental capacity to be completed effectively. The amount of capacity needed changes depending on the stage of learning. Novices need to use all of this resource just to be able to hit the ball. As a result, the novice can only focus on hitting the ball. The expert (for whom the skill has become automatic) can execute the skill and focus on the outside world (e.g., field settings and gaps in the field).

Now, let's say that in each case these tasks take 100% of this focusing capacity; nothing more, nothing less. In both cases the novice and the expert will be able to perform their associated tasks. However, if the capacity for an individual decreases to 90% of the overall capacity then all of a sudden the player doesn't have enough capacity for the task. Once this happens something has to be left out. For the novice it ends up being an aspect of the technique they are trying to execute, and for the expert it is their awareness of the field (increasing the possibility of them playing the ball to the fielder). The question remains though, 'why would this happen?' Well, there are three main factors that could cause this reduction in focusing capacity: stress, over arousal, and tiredness.

All three of these factors have similar impacts upon your focusing capacity. So, as you become more stressed (experiencing negative emotions) your capacity to focus will decrease, which is one of the reasons why controlling your emotions is crucial in cricket. Also, if you become too worked up and the 'red mist' descends, a similar reduction in your focusing capacity will occur. Finally, as you become more tired (both physically and mentally) your focusing capacity again decreases.

Each of these things on their own is not great, but a combination of these factors can be catastrophic. This also highlights another important factor when considering the mental side of the game. While we discuss many of the psychological factors separately they *often exist together*. As a result they can interact to further increase the impact they have. In this case, an inability to control your emotions can lead to a decrease in your ability to focus. As this emotionality continues it also makes you more tired, which also has the knock on effect of further reducing your ability to focus. All of which can potentially lead to a catastrophic fall in performance.

The best way to stop yourself from being affected by distractions, or letting the pressure of the situation affect you, and to stop focusing taking up too much of your mental energy is to have specific strategies of *what* to focus on, and importantly *when* to focus.

Strategies to Enhance Focus

The main principle behind focusing strategies is very simple. As discussed previously, with an ability to only think about one thing at a time, if you are deliberately thinking of one thing (e.g., watch the ball) it is very unlikely that you will be easily distracted. There are exceptions to this. For example, if someone nearby says your name, and you hear them, you will usually switch your attention to that person. The implication of this is that if you were looking to distract someone you would probably make sure that you said their name!

All focusing strategies work by following this simple principle. The main techniques used in cricket relate to:

- Developing a pre-delivery routine
- Using cue words
- Using triggers
- Setting specific task-specific goals

Another very effective yet simple technique is to just focus on your breathing. Many players develop strategies that incorporate a number of these approaches, whereas other players just adopt a simple approach. It really is a case of finding out what works best for you.

Focusing Routines

Pre-delivery routines are a consistent feature in almost all aspects of cricket. Watch any game of cricket and you will probably observe that the batsman does the same things before facing each delivery (e.g., checking their gloves, touching their pads, tapping their bat at the crease, or marking middle stump), the bowler will have some consistent behaviours (spinning the ball from one hand to another, or always turning the same way at the end of their run up) and the keeper will have some consistent movements (check gloves in a specific order then crouching).

Chapter 3

Usually this is a natural process where we look to prepare the same way to execute our skills. In the same way, the best players have a consistent pre-delivery *mental routine* alongside the actions and behaviours that prepare them to perform. The big advantage to this is that if you are focusing on your routine, then you are unlikely to be distracted.

The second big advantage to a routine is that it will also offer a natural 'trigger' to either begin focusing, or to refocus (recognising you can't focus with the same intensity all of the time).

The individual components of the routine are actually not that important, although it does help if these components relate to what you are about to do (execute your skills). At the same time we need to remember that we do not want to be thinking very technical things as this will ultimately stop us executing our skills effectively (paralysis by analysis). The ideal approach would be to develop consistent thoughts that link with the behaviours that already exist as part of a player's preparations.

So, it could be that the batsman's routine involves setting their stance, checking their balance, preparing to face the delivery, and then watching the ball. A very simple mental routine would involve saying "*Stance, balance, prepare, watch the ball*". To be very effective this should be linked into the timing of the behaviours, so saying "*Stance*" as you set your stance, and "*balance*" as you check your balance, and so on. The things that you say (in your head) or think can be anything that works for you, but the important bit is that they are *consistent*. That said though there are always exceptions. We can think of numerous examples of very successful professional and international cricketers who have either sung a song in their head or, in one case, just counted as quickly as he could.

As mentioned at the start, the strategy used is not the most important thing, it's *consistent application in practice* is key. The fact that it focuses the mind and works for the individual player is the crucial part. This ultimately means that using and learning the routine in practice, so you can then apply it more consistently in a game, is the way to achieve the best results. (See *Chapter Nine* for further details of how to practice to perform).

A central part of Australian batsman Justin Langer's routine was to watch the ball, whereas Australian fast bowler Brett Lee highlighted how he "...*often got back to the top of my mark and 'visioned' in my mind the next delivery, it would be the ball I wanted to bowl. Amazing feeling when it would come off!"*

One way in which pre-delivery routines can be developed is an approach that was adopted in developing routines for professional players. In one example, a sport psychologist worked with a batsman and bowler at the same professional club. Both of the players had approached the sport psychologist during the off-season specifically looking for strategies to enhance their ability to focus during the game and to know when to switch on and off.

The two players highlighted specific issues regarding what to think about during this initial stage of their preparation to perform. While both of the players had very consistent behavioural routines they did not really have any concrete mental components to their pre-delivery preparation. As a result, various unhelpful thought processes such as thinking about the future, dwelling on the past, or just being negative about themselves took place.

The sport psychologist sought to develop individualized pre-delivery routines based on the following:

- The specific requirements of the skill that they were executing
- The pre-existing behaviours (what they currently did)
- The players' preferred mindset
- What the players wanted to achieve at the end of their routines

The first step involved checking what they thought the function of their pre-delivery routine should be (e.g., making effective decisions, focusing, relaxing). This approach also reflects the fact that it is important to build any pre-delivery routine around the needs of the individual player. As such, no two routines should be exactly the same. The existing behaviours were exactly that, the things that they already did. The sport psychologist videoed each player in the nets then looked to see what actions and behaviours were always present in the pre-delivery period. This is important as trying to 'unlearn' habitual behaviours when skills have become automatic is very time consuming and in some cases you can never fully change these existing behaviours. It is better to work with what is already there.

Once the actions/behaviours had been identified, each player stated what they wanted their PDR to achieve (e.g., relaxation, focusing, increased arousal levels). The next step sought to clarify exactly what function each of these actions/behaviours fulfilled. So, if the player marked a line on the pitch (like Jonathan Trott does when he is batting for England) what was the reason for this? What function did it fulfil? This step involved the players doing their existing behaviours in a practice environment, then after each ball was bowled or faced, discussing with the sport psychologist what each of the behaviours meant and what functions the player felt that it served.

Players were also encouraged to discuss any existing mental strategies that they used in conjunction with the highlighted behaviours. Based on this information relevant cue words (the mental component) were developed that linked to the player's behaviours (the physical component).

Once all of this was completed the final step involved the player practicing the new routine in training to make it a habit. To make this happen the players were first asked to go through the physical parts of their routine while saying the mental components out loud. This approach sought to fulfil three main requirements:

1. For the players to 'learn' the mental components of the routines
2. To create a link between the behaviours and the mental components
3. To make sure that the players were using the routines for each separate delivery (not just when asked)

Once this had been practiced the next step was to remove the think aloud aspect, recognizing that saying the thoughts can be disruptive to performing the skill. This process was repeated on a number of separate occasions with the sport psychologist and coach present. The players then continued to integrate this process into all of their practice sessions. The main aim here was to work towards creating a routine that became habit, which further complemented the existing behaviours.

Discussions with the coaching staff who worked with the players also reinforced the continued learning and practice of the routines. The coaches specifically made reference to the developed routines for the players in each practice net session. The pre-delivery routines were well received by both the professional players. Both reported feeling comfortable with their routines six weeks after initial development.

This approach can be used, to a greater or lesser extent, by any cricketer. It offers a clear process to develop a pre-delivery routine that is relevant and individualised to enable them to perform most effectively. For further details see Resource 3.1 at the end of this chapter.

Cue Words

Cue words are words or sayings that you use to get yourself to respond in a certain way. Cue words can be used as a motivational tool (e.g., come on, you can do it), or can be used to give you a specific focus (e.g., watch the ball).

Cue words can be used as components of a pre-delivery routine (see the previous section) or as the ball is being bowled to focus your mind. As with the other strategies discussed here, the cue words used are a very personal thing. Indeed to be most effective they need to work for the individual player. So feel free to ask other players what they do, and read about what successful players have used to help them. Make sure you use something that feels comfortable for you.

There are no right or wrong approaches, as long as cue words are consistently applied and practiced. You can say something related to the task at hand (e.g., play it straight), something related to how you feel (e.g., just relax), or something unrelated (e.g., oranges); if it works and feels comfortable then it works! The key, just like with the other strategies in this book, is using the strategy consistently and practicing it when in the nets and doing drills (not just in the games).

There is also a link between what you think and what you do. So it is better to focus on what you *should do* rather than what *not to do*. Focusing on what not to do is something the brain struggles with. It is only really good at responding to instructions of what to do. If you focus on something you shouldn't do, your brain can get confused and do the very thing you have been trying to avoid. So make sure you are saying something you should be doing!

Triggers

A trigger is exactly what you think it would be. A word, or thought, or behaviour that serves as a marker so you know it is time to focus or refocus. These triggers can either be behaviours or thoughts (or a combination of the two). Again, it is something that you consistently do that tells you that it is time to focus again.

Sometimes (but not always) it might be the start of your pre-delivery routine, but a trigger could also be something that you say to yourself when you realise you are not focused (come on, focus on the game). Again, to be most effective you should have a strategy that you use for every delivery. This is because you should be focusing effectively every ball (regardless of whether you are the batsman, the bowler, the keeper, or a fielder).

To start with, as you practice this trigger, it will feel a little strange, but like with your skills, practice will make the technique permanent. Practice will also move the strategy from being something you have to think about to something that you just do (allowing you to refocus for each delivery without having to think about focusing). An example of your trigger might be getting the ball in your hands as a bowler, or checking your gloves as a wicket keeper. It is just a behaviour (something you do) that tells you *it is time* for the next ball and to re-focus.

Self-Talk

For some players just using a single word or phrase (cue words) is not enough. They like to have more explicit conversations with themselves. In some cases you can see these players talking to themselves, but often this chatter takes place just in their head. If you adopt this approach you will probably have general themes for things you talk to yourself about, but not necessarily a fixed script of words that you consistently say time after time.

Self-talk works along the same lines as the other strategies in this section. If you are focusing on what you are saying you do not have the spare capacity to think about other things. As such it can be an effective tool to shut out distractions. Justin Langer was an advocate of self-talk. He highlighted the impact that this 'chatter' in your head can have: *"If I want to give myself the best chance of success in anything I do, I have to talk to myself. Negative self-talk is extremely destructive, positive self-talk on the other hand, is one of the keys to success."* Justin Langer's comments clearly illustrate how positive self-talk can enhance performance, and how negative self-talk can serve as a distraction and have the opposite effect.

Goal-Setting

Another technique that you might use, if you feel that you need to think about more than just a cue word, is setting particular goals. Goals are useful as they are specific and related to your performance, but are not too technical (so will not stop you being able to execute your skills). Also, from a focusing point of view, if you are thinking about your goal, then you are not letting your mind wander or allowing yourself to be distracted.

As with the other techniques this one is down to personal preference. You might opt to have a consistent goal for the game (e.g., stay relaxed, or play straight) or you might change your goals (per ball, per over, or in blocks of overs). As suggested before, it is all down to personal preference. It is down to what feels most comfortable for you.

Whatever focusing technique or approach you ultimately opt for - the most important aspect is to practice it. Under pressure we revert back to our habitual (well learnt) responses. So, you need to make sure that your focusing strategy becomes one of your habits when playing cricket. The only effective way to do this is to make sure that the technique you use is well learnt, and this only happens through lots of repetition and practice.

To make your focusing strategy as effective as possible you need to make sure that you use it not just every time you play a game, but every time that you practice. So, if you have developed a pre-delivery routine when batting you need to use the routine every time you face a ball in the nets. Through this process the routine will become second nature and as a result you will begin to use the routine even when you are not thinking about it.

One final point on practice is that generally, deliberately practicing these techniques will feel a little awkward to start with, but you need to persevere. The focusing technique will begin to feel less awkward and then eventually you will stop being aware that you are using the technique; but it will still be doing its job in giving your mind a specific focus when playing or bowling a delivery. It will also give you that clear guide for when to switch on, and when to switch off. This should ensure that you are completely focused when you need to be, and able to switch off that intense focus off when you can (breaks in play, in between deliveries). You will become able to switch it back on when you need to.

Justin Langer used to use what he referred to as 'white noise' to help him to concentrate. This worked on the basis of humming a tune or imagining specific therapeutic sounds. Langer clarified the use of white noise by saying that *"White noise is just another form of concentration. I'm often asked what it's like to play in front of huge crowds, while the world's media and millions of viewers are watching your every move. If I exist only in the moment then there is no room in my mind for any distraction."* This reinforces the view that almost anything can work if used effectively by the player.

Summary

Knowing what to focus on, and when to focus, is crucial to being successful as a cricketer. It might be that normally you are fine and don't get distracted but when you get to that big game, where there is a lot of pressure and stress all of a sudden, you find you can't focus and spend too much time dwelling on the past or fortune telling (thinking about the future).

The best players perform well in these situations because they already have well developed and well learnt strategies. This way, whilst it is a big game, or big over, or important last ball, you are able to just focus on the next delivery and not get distracted by the external environment (e.g., the crowd, the opposition, the scoreboard) or the internal environment (such as thinking about how important the situation is). You have already occupied your mind with your routine, goals, cue words, or triggers. If you just try and use something when you get to the big games it won't work. You need to have practiced a routine and ensured it is well learnt.

Remember, you can only focus on one thing at a time, so make sure it is the one that gives you the greatest opportunity to execute your skills - ball after ball after ball.

Key messages:

- You are always focusing on something
- Focusing takes effort and energy, so focusing intensely for periods of time will make you tired
- Tiredness, and emotionality, decrease your ability to focus
- You can get distracted by both internal and external factors
- You need to develop strategies to occupy your mind to stop you from becoming distracted. Allow yourself to just execute your skills

Further reading:

Langer, J. (2008). *Seeing the Sun Rise*. Crows Nest, NSW: Allen & Unwin.

Advanced reading:

Cotterill, S. T. (2010). Pre-performance routines in sport: Current understanding and future directions. *International Review of Sport & Exercise Psychology*, 3, 132-153.

Cotterill, S. T. (2011). Experiences of developing pre-performance routines with elite cricket players. *Journal of Sport Psychology in Action*, 2, 81-91.

Moran, A. (1996). *The psychology of concentration in sport performers: A cognitive analysis*. Hove: Psychological Press.

Chapter 3

Focusing Resources

Resource 3.1, Developing a pre-delivery routine.

In seeking to develop an effective pre-delivery routine follow these six steps:

1. Understand what you want your routine to achieve (i.e., is it to focus, to relax, to control your emotions, to think).

2. Understand current behaviours (ideally through videoing your preparation, but if not - get someone to observe you and make a note of what you do, and in what order).

3. Clarify the meaning of current behaviours (look at all the things you do, highlighted in the previous step, and see if they help you to achieve the things you want from step 1).

4. Develop a function and focus for each behavioural component (for each behaviour make sure you have an associated thought that helps you to achieve the things highlighted in step 1; e.g., setting your stance helps you balance, checking your grip helps you relax).

5. Build the new routine (make sure you have a 'thought' for each of the behaviours that you keep in your routine. The easiest way is to have a word / action that you think for each bit; e.g., stance, balance, relax, watch the ball).

6. Practice using the new routine - all the time! (you need to practice how you are going to play, so once you have a routine you need to use it for every practice delivery; you want it to become habit for the real thing).

4

Performing Under Pressure

"Cricket is a pressure game." Imran Khan

The above words from Imran Khan are accurate in many ways. You can probably recall an important game that you played where you were out in the middle, alone, facing difficult deliveries on a less than perfect wicket, chasing a score that seemed unreachable, but a score that you were expected to reach by spectators, your teammates, your coach, and you.

Or a time when you were sitting in the changing rooms before a crucial must-win game; perhaps you were alone with your thoughts, preparing to go out and compete, your mind riddled with worries and doubts, your body tense, your stomach queasy, your heart beating out of your chest.

These are common experiences but the quote from Imran Khan does not paint the whole picture, and does not tell us the entire story. Pressure is a perception of a situation, not a situation itself. In other words, cricket, just like all other sports, is made pressured by the way we think about demanding situations like an important game, or that 'unreachable' runs target. This is very important because it means that our thoughts determine how much pressure we experience.

If we change the way we think about demanding situations, we can alter our experience of pressure. It is not fully accurate to describe cricket as pressured, and it is not accurate to say that important games make us feel pressured. It is more accurate to instead recognize that cricket is very demanding, but it is how we *think* about cricket that makes us feel pressured.

"I don't really let pressure affect me at all. I believe that pressure is something that an individual creates for himself and it's something that you can avoid. I just go out there, relax, smile, enjoy myself, play my

natural game, do what comes naturally to me and play my cricket according to the conditions and match situation. The more you worry about things when you are out there in the middle, the more problems you are going to encounter." Mohammad Amir (who made his first One-Day International and Test appearance in 2009 at the age of 17).

The good news is that you can change the way you think in order to cope better with demanding situations, and there are many other ways that you can learn to deal with pressure (which we will spend some time on later in this chapter).

In the first part of this chapter we discuss why pressure can be bad for performance, why the ability to cope under pressure is such an important part of becoming and thriving as a professional cricketer, and explore the idea that pressure is not always necessarily harmful for performance.

"I reckon I have put a lot of pressure on myself to perform... I have not been able to deal with it as well of late as I would have liked to. Normally for me when those big moments come around I have been able to find something within and go out and score runs. I have not been able to do that for a while now and that was when the alarm bells started to ring." Ricky Ponting on his retirement.

Why can Pressure be so Bad?

In cricket, as in all sports, performance will fluctuate. This is normal and inescapable, as even the greats have bad days. Sometimes we perform a bit better than normal, and sometimes a bit worse. But there is a phenomenon that occurs only under *perceived* pressure that can disrupt performance so dramatically and suddenly, it is referred to by many as *choking*.

What distinguishes choking from normal variations in performance is that choking refers to performance that is much worse than expected given a cricketer's skill level, and when the incentives for optimal performance are at a maximum. In other words, choking happens when performance matters most.

Choking can be sudden, for example being dismissed for a golden duck facing a delivery that you would normally be quite comfortable with. Choking can also last for a while, for example bowling no ball after no ball throughout an entire over (see Scott Boswell's 14-ball over for Leicestershire against Somerset in the C&G Trophy final in 2001). But why does choking occur and what is it about perceived pressure that causes choking?

Thinking too much

Psychologists have recognized for a long time that one of the main reasons athletes choke is because they over-think the situation and more specifically, over-think skill execution.

As skilled performers, elite cricketers have trained extremely hard to build and cement core skills into their games. Day after day, week after week, repeating batting strokes, and or ball deliveries, so that in the heat of a game, they have the technical skills to produce complex skills with relative ease. In fact, many elite cricketers can execute skills in such a manner that it feels automatic, as if they are on autopilot. Great! All that training has paid off.

But something happens to many athletes when under pressure. Instead of letting their skills flow naturally, they start to think about their skills, and spend mental resources trying to control the little parts that make up that skill. Victory is so important, but in demanding games victory is under threat, so many athletes respond by taking extra care to execute their skills and analyze their execution to make sure its spot on. Herein lies the problem.

Once a skill is well learned, there is no need to think about the little parts that make the skill happen, and in doing so, skill execution can actually get worse! By bringing that well learned (implicit) skill under conscious control, athletes are drawing on explicit knowledge that disrupts the mechanics of the skill. For example, explicit knowledge may include your exact foot movements, body positioning, timing of your stroke, and even your hand positioning on the bat. A cricketer can go from his normal smooth and natural ground stroke, to an uncoordinated swing at the ball.

Chapter 4

Professor Sian Beilock, who is a leading expert on choking, refers to the phenomenon as 'paralysis by analysis' (see also *Chapter Three*), and later in this chapter we will discuss ways to guard against this powerful performance disruptor. Paralysis by analysis is not the only way pressure can cause choking, so now we move on to an intriguing and equally dangerous phenomenon called ironic processes of mental control.

Don't mess up!

It seems so obvious. You are the cricketer of choice for your team when it comes to batting for long periods of time. They can rely on you to build an innings, sap the energy out of opponents, and soak up overs like a sponge. It's the final day of the test, and again your job is to stay in.

As you pad-up and prepare, you feel nervous, this is an importance game. Your coach says three simple words to you that have been the curse of many an elite athlete: "*Don't mess up.*" These words ring and echo in your mind as you walk out onto the field to your crease, "*Don't mess up, whatever you do don't get out.*" As you step into the crease for the first ball you remind yourself, "*Don't let the moment get to you, whatever you do don't mess up.*" Then relative silence as the bowler takes his run up. The next sounds you hear are the cheers of your opponents and your inner voice asking "*What happened?*"

So what did happen? Surely in this situation - telling yourself not to get out is a good plan. It seems obvious; telling yourself not to get out will surely reduce the likelihood of getting out.

Unfortunately, Professor Daniel M. Wegner has discovered that the exact opposite is true: telling yourself not to do something increases the likelihood of doing it. Try it now. Don't think of a white bear. Whatever you do don't think of a white bear. Chances are you are now thinking about what I told you not to think about. So why does this happen? Why, when we tell ourselves not to do or think about something, does it ironically increase the likelihood of doing and thinking about that thing? See Figure 4.1 for how ironic processes might disrupt cricket performance.

Figure 4.1, The effect of ironic processing on cricket performance.

The reason for ironic processing has to do with the way your mind works under pressure. The attempt to not think about something triggers two mental processes, one conscious process (in your awareness) that searches for anything to think about *other than* the unwanted thought (e.g., getting out). The other mental process is automatic (outside of your awareness) and searches for the unwanted thought.

So, when trying not to think about getting out, the conscious process leads to thoughts about things that might distract you from the thought of getting out (such as match tactics, the weather, or the surface of the wicket). In other words, you deliberately think about things that override the idea of getting out. But at the same time, the automatic mental process keeps searching for the unwanted thought and alerts you when it finds the unwanted thought. Because the automatic mental process is relentless and keeps searching, it increases the chances of that unwanted thought resurfacing into your conscious awareness.

Now here is the problem when we add pressure into the mix. Commonly, when under pressure, athletes worry about their performance, and usually the consequences of failure. This worrying uses up mental capacity (or space) that you need for the conscious process (the one that distracts you from the unwanted thought) to be effective. With the conscious process rendered ineffective by worry, the unconscious process takes over and successfully searches and finds the unwanted thoughts you were trying so hard to avoid!

So, especially in circumstances where your mind is full of worry, when you are feeling pressured, these ironic processes take over, leading you to think and act in ways that are directly opposed to your goals. Later in the chapter we will discuss how to guard against letting these ironic processes disrupt performance, but for now we will consider what happens to our concentration when under pressure.

Focusing on the wrong things

"Any active sportsman has to be very focused; you've got to be in the right frame of mind. If your energy is diverted in various directions, you do not achieve the results." Sachin Tendulkar

Performing under pressure can also influence how cricketers attend to cues in the environment. Many cricketers experience a narrowing of their concentration span meaning that they can't take in all the information available in the environment. This is often called tunnel vision. Tunnel vision is a double edged sword in cricket. On the one hand, under pressure we have a tendency to focus on the most 'threatening' parts of the environment which are often task-irrelevant. This could be the score board, the crowd, or even the sledging aimed at you before deliveries.

Focusing on these task-irrelevant aspects is not likely to help you perform at your best. On the flip side, tunnel vision can be beneficial in blocking out these task-irrelevant cues if you are able to focus only on the relevant cues that are more likely to help you perform at your best. For example, only focusing on the ball from the beginning of the bowler's run up, all the way to your bat. Under pressure, using this tunnel vision to focus on an aspect that is important for success achieves two main things.

1. It allows you to block out potential distractions (e.g., task irrelevant aspects).
2. By using an external focus such as the ball, it means you are not focusing on the mechanics of the skill or your own thoughts. Therefore, you are less likely to fall victim to paralysis by analysis (over thinking the mechanics of the skill) or unwanted thoughts (*"Don't mess up!"*).

Later, we will discuss ways to focus on the right things, but now we move on to looking at how your body responds to pressure.

Feeling Threatened

"Every time when I go to the crease and prepare to face the first ball, I am nervous and there are butterflies in my tummy." Virender Sehwag

Most athletes will talk about experiencing a constellation of physical feelings when under pressure. These often include butterflies like Virender Sehwag describes, or a host of other symptoms such as:

- Sweaty palms
- Tense muscles
- Nausea
- Lethargy

Or, in contrast:

- Hyperactivity
- Restlessness

The first, and highly important, point is that these feelings are normal and are part of what we call a 'stress response'. Stress responses occur in all manner of important situations not just cricket competition.

When faced with demanding situations such as competition, your brain very quickly makes a decision on what the situation means to you, and what kind of response is needed. Based on this decision, which often happens without you even being aware of it, the heart beats faster and hormones are released into the blood and circulated round the body. This is crucial for performance as this response rapidly delivers oxygen and energy to the areas of the body that need it most, such as the muscles and the brain. As well as speeding up the delivery of oxygen and energy, this response also gives rise to the physical symptoms you may experience before an important game (e.g., tension, racing heart). Our brain has been programmed over millions of years of evolution to respond in this way, and rapidly to demanding situations. Sounds great so far.

However, there are two different ways that we can respond to stress; one good for performance, one bad. These two responses have been called challenge and threat states (see Figure 4.2), and our research has shown that cricketers that respond to a demanding situation in a threat state perform *worse* than those who respond in a challenge state.

To explain, in our laboratory we informed cricketers about an upcoming pressured batting test they would be taking, requiring them to chase 36 runs from 30 deliveries against a pace bowling machine. As the cricketers were informed about the pressure test we recorded their cardiovascular responses and asked them some questions about their thoughts and feelings. We found that cricketers who displayed increased Vascular Resistance (constriction in blood vessels) and decreased Cardiac Output (amount of blood pumped from the heart per minute), which we call a threat state, performed poorly in the pressured batting test.

In contrast, cricketers who displayed decreased Vascular Resistance and increased Cardiac Output, which we call a challenge state, performed well in the pressured batting test. In other words, how the cricketers' cardiovascular systems responded to *approaching* the pressure test predicted how well they did when they *actually* performed the test. We have found the same results in a number of mental and physical tasks, with athletes involved in all kinds of sports.

A challenge state leads to better performance than a threat state; but why? There are two main reasons why this could be the case. First, a challenge state reflects a positive psychological approach to performance, and we know that if an athlete feels confident, in control, and focuses on what he/she can achieve, performance is less likely to be disrupted under pressure. Athletes in a challenge state are also less likely to over-think their performance and less likely to experience unwanted thoughts, which as we have discussed earlier, are major causes of choking under pressure. There is more on how to increase your own confidence, feelings of control, and achievement goals, later in this chapter.

Second, the cardiovascular responses displayed in a challenge state reflect an efficient physiological response to pressure compared to a threat state. Because in a challenge state Vascular Resistance decreases and Cardiac Output increases, blood can quickly and efficiently get to the areas of the body that really need it for performance. Blood carries oxygen and energy to the muscles and the brain so you can perform physically and mentally (e.g., attention and emotion control) under pressure. The more efficient this process is, the more likely you are to perform well. So in a threat state, because Vascular Resistance increases and Cardiac Output decreases, it is a less efficient response, and therefore performance is more likely to be disrupted.

Figure 4.2, The mental, physiological, and performance aspects of challenge and threat states.

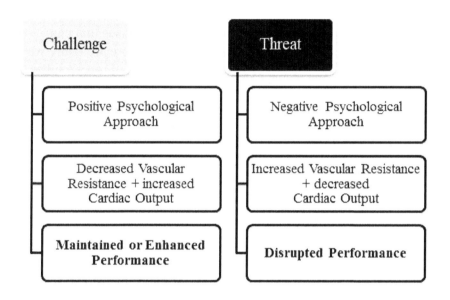

It's not all bad news if you respond to pressure in a threat state. Cricketers who maintain high levels of confidence and focus on what they can achieve, rather than trying to avoid failure, can display a threat state but still perform well under pressure. Therefore, first and foremost it is important to be confident and to focus on the right things (e.g., what you *can* do to perform well) to promote a challenge state and inoculate against a threat state, and to help you fulfill your potential. Remember, pressure can be good as long you get your mental approach right, as James Anderson suggests below.

"I thrive on pressure now…In the past, maybe, the pressure might have got to me…But now it's more exciting. You want to play in big games. You want to test yourself against the best in the world." James Anderson, 18th July, 2012.

Chapter 4

So now we know what it is about pressure that can harm performance. We know that it is how we *think* about demanding situations that causes pressure. Pressure is perceived not received. Based on the *perception* of pressure, we can either respond well, for example in a challenge state, or negatively, for example in a threat state. If we focus on the wrong things, such as avoiding failure, over-analyzing skill execution, and trying to suppress unwanted thoughts, we are likely to choke when it matters most.

How we respond to pressure can cause bodily responses that can influence performance too. As we have gathered, there are many ways in which pressure can harm performance. But, years of research has produced effective mental skills and psychological techniques to help athletes respond well to pressure. Also, in our own sport psychology practice we have developed numerous strategies to help cricketers to fulfill their potential in those situations where being at your best is vital. So, next, we move on to outline some of the skills you can learn and use to help you thrive under pressure.

Thriving Under Pressure

Thinking Smart

We have already come to terms with the idea that pressure is based on our perceptions of upcoming events or situations and therefore, like all perceptions, can be altered and changed. By changing the way you think about upcoming situations it is possible to reduce and control the amount of pressure you put on yourself.

The importance of an upcoming event is one of the major causes of perceptions of pressure. We have all been in situations of great importance where success could improve our lives and failure could mean we miss out on extremely desirable victor's spoils. Often, especially at an academy level, failures could mean de-selection and too often this can lead to cricketers dropping out of the sport all together.

So it would be a good idea to *reduce* the perceived importance of the event, right? Well not quite. It is, in part, the importance of the event that brings the best out of cricketers. In fact, if you think back to some of your best performances, they were probably in situations of great importance. Think back to your favourite athlete's best performance, again it probably occurred in a critical international match of some sort. So 'pretending' that the event is not important may reduce pressure, but may also take away that edge that you often need to produce your best. As the below quote from Sachin Tendulkar suggests, it may be best to treat each match as importantly as the last.

"*My point of view is that when I am playing cricket I cannot think that this game is less or more important.*" Sachin Tendulkar

It is possible to reduce perceptions of pressure without altering the importance of the event. We call it "Smarter Thinking" and it involves the vital skill of putting success and failure into perspective, using realistic and logical reasoning.

In our own work we have found that before important matches athletes often place demands on themselves that are unrealistic and illogical. For example, "*I must succeed*", "*I have to play well today*", or "*I must not play poorly today*". By using such rigid demands as "*I must succeed*" before an important match, perceptions of pressure are quite easily inflamed. The reason for this is simple. Giving yourself such a strict inflexible demand *increases the importance* of the event beyond *reasonable proportions*. It makes failure too threatening, and this can create pressure so intense that performance suffers in the ways we discussed earlier in the chapter.

One of the best ways to change these rigid beliefs is to gain some perspective. First, spend a few minutes thinking about the things you truly *must* have in life. Do this before you continue to read on.

Good. You probably have a mental list of five to eight things. This list may include water, air, food, sleep, and other kinds of life or death things. That is what *must* means after all; to be compelled, as by a physical necessity or requirement. Does success in cricket really fit in with these vital necessities? Not quite. But by believing that you must succeed, you are suggesting that success in cricket does fit in with the list of necessities. You can see how this would create added pressure.

Another strategy you can use is to *think logically* about the rigid demand. For example, where is it written that you must succeed? Does it follow that just because you want to succeed, and that success would be highly favourable, that you must?

Finally, have you failed in the past? We are guessing, like us, you probably have failed many times in the past. By having previous failures you automatically disprove your rigid demands for success. How can you say *"I must succeed"* when you can think of times when you haven't succeeded? Again, think of your favourite athlete. Now recall their failures, and think back to times when they have underperformed when it mattered. For example, on his Test debut in 1975 against the touring Australia side Graham Gooch got a pair, and Shane Warne on his Test debut in 1992 against India took 1/150 off 45 overs. Even the greats go against the demand for success.

Apologies for our questioning style. But in our experience it is best to leave the rigid and demanding ways of thinking behind and replace them with much more flexible alternatives, and the first step to achieving this is to understand that words like 'must' really have little place in sport. Take, for example, what Roy Hodgson, the England Football manager, said prior to a World Cup qualifier in October 2012:

"It's an important moment. But it's a game of football, a game we've worked hard to prepare for and a game, if we win, that can give us a very good start to our qualifying campaign...But after 36 years the words "must win" leave me rather cold. Most teams go on the field wanting to win. I don't know how you achieve a "must win" other than going out to try and play."

So it is possible to maintain the importance of a match. It is possible to prepare the best you can, to exert maximum effort trying to succeed, and to let your desire to win drive you, without placing rigid demands on yourself. It is okay to want to succeed more than anything else in the world, and it may be true that some matches might be the most important events you have ever performed in. But the desire to perform well in an important match does not mean that you "must" perform well. The 'must' only inflames the pressure.

One way to protect against such rigid beliefs is to remind yourself of logical and flexible beliefs often, and especially before important matches. You can write logical statements down on cue cards to help motivate yourself and to remind you to keep perspective and not put too much pressure on yourself. Here are some we have written to give you an example:

- ✓ *"I want to succeed more than anything, but that doesn't mean I must."*
- ✓ *"It is really important for me to perform well, but it won't be the end of the world if I fail."*
- ✓ *"Today's match is so important, and I want more than anything to play well."*

The previous statements are logical, reasonable, and flexible. They also reflect the desire to succeed and recognise the importance of performing well. What we are not trying to do is reduce the importance of the event, or pretend the event doesn't matter. Remember, some pressure can be good for your performance, but too much can make you choke. Control your perceptions of pressure by gaining perspective and adopting flexible beliefs. By gaining some perspective on what success and failure in cricket really means to you, and by thinking smartly about how you approach important events, you can experience more helpful perceptions of pressure for your performance.

'See' yourself cope

"I had to psyche myself into seeing the packed stadium, the Australian team waiting in the middle along with the two umpires. I also had to imagine my partner, Virender Sehwag, was walking alongside me. Then I did my ritual, running a couple of mock runs, before settling in to take strike. I mentally drew a line just outside the off stump, to use as a marker for letting balls go. Anything pitched outside that line would be allowed to go through to the keeper and the rest were to be played. Then I'd stand in my stance and visualise all the Australian bowlers running in and bowling in different areas. It is a routine I've followed ever since." Aakash Chopra, 24th September, 2009.

One of the important factors you may notice about the above quote from Aakash Chopra is how much detail he creates in his mind about the *type* of situation he is performing in. He talks about the packed stadium, his opponents waiting, all of his opponents bowling at him in a variety of areas. In other words, he creates a demanding situation in his mind. He creates a perception of pressure by very realistically visualising being in an important and difficult situation. Surely this doesn't make sense? Why would an athlete imagine performing in situations where they may be uncomfortable, and where the chances of failure are increased?

There is good evidence to suggest that visualising oneself coping under pressure in demanding situations improves future responses to pressure. That is, by realistically imagining yourself in a demanding match situation and seeing yourself perform well, with control and composure despite being uncomfortable, you can more confidently approach actual important matches in the same way; controlled and composed.

Imagery or visualisation is a fascinating phenomenon especially when it comes to pressure. By imagining demanding situations as realistically as you can, the brain starts to respond in a similar way to if you were actually facing a demanding situation.

If you are able to 'see' what you would see in an actual situation, 'hear' the same sounds, and 'feel' the same things, then you can recreate the mental and physical responses that are experienced in actual demanding situations. This gives the brain and the body a glimpse of what to expect in actual performance situations, and therefore better prepares you for those all-important matches.

So, if you visualise coping in your realistically imagined pressure situation, it is like rehearsing your desired response. If you want to be controlled and composed under pressure, then imagine being so. Think of it as creating a *mental blueprint* of how to respond under pressure.

You can test your ability to create pressure perceptions in your head. Earlier we talked about the physical symptoms of pressure: sweaty palms, racing heart, butterflies. When you imagine demanding situations, the brain starts to respond in a similar way to how it would respond in actual demanding situations and the body follows suit. So strap a heart rate monitor to your chest or your wrist and try to imagine preparing to compete in a really important match.

First, get nice and relaxed. When fully relaxed take a look at the heart rate monitor and make a note of the reading. Then close your eyes and imagine sitting in the changing rooms waiting to go out and perform in a really important match. Remember to create sights, sounds, feelings, and even smells! Make it more specific to you by using a real upcoming match perhaps. When you feel that the script is causing you to feel pressure, take a look at the heart rate monitor and make a note of the reading. You will probably notice that your heart rate has increased. Remember, this is a normal and very sensitive physiological response to perceptions of pressure; a response that helps you to prepare mentally and physically for the demands of performance. You can repeat this exercise on the morning of an important match, for example, and if you know exactly where you are playing and who your opponents will be, just like Aakash Chopra, you can make the imagery ever more realistic.

Visualisation can be used in many other ways, for example to control your emotions and to help you relax in those pressure moments. If you want to know more about visualisation you may wish to read *Chapter Seven* on *Controlling Your Emotions* in this book.

Focusing on the right things

In our experience, much of the mental side of cricket is making sure the mind is focused on what you can do to perform well, rather than what you can do to avoid failure.

It may be helpful to think of the mind, in performance situations, as an empty vessel that you'd better fill up with helpful thoughts - leaving no room for unhelpful thoughts. If you are busy focusing on the key parts of your performance, then you aren't able to focus on doubts, concerns, and possible failure. In other words, before you perform, you only need to focus on what you need to do to succeed; everything else is a waste of time and space.

The strategy we use with cricketers to help with this skill is to get them to think of the *three most important* aspects of their performance going into a particular match. Then we get them to write these three things down. These need to be controllable and acute. For example, it's no good having "*scoring 150 runs*" as this isn't really controllable (to an extent) and would happen over a long period of time. Good examples are: hitting the gaps in the field, defending your wicket, and being positive in all actions.

Chapter 4

Using their visualisation skills the player then runs these aspects over in his/her head over and over again, usually while walking out to bat. So, they might imagine:

- Hitting gaps in the field off many different deliveries in many different gaps
- Defending the wicket strongly (even when facing difficult deliveries)
- Imagining a range of strokes performed positively and perfectly

No stroke should be visualised as a half-hearted attempt, all strokes should be positive and meaningful!

The way in which these three aspects are imagined can vary. It can be a mix of shots and images, or you can imagine hitting the gaps ten times, then defending your wicket ten times, then being positive ten times. Or you may wish to use 'rewind' and 'fast forward' functions in your mind for the shots - as if you are experiencing a highlight reel of your future performance. The most important thing to remember, if you use this strategy, is that you focus on the things you need to do to perform well. Leave no space in your mental approach for doubts and concerns (see Figure 4.3).

Figure 4.3, The effect of focusing on helpful thoughts.

"My best moments as a batsman came when I had no extraneous thoughts in my head. It was about having a clear focus, concentrating wholly on the next ball and playing it as best I could." Steve Waugh in his 2005 Autobiography.

Oh, the irony

Earlier, we talked about a phenomenon call ironic processing. To recap, when under pressure, attempts to *not think,* or *not do* something, increases the likelihood of thinking and doing that very thing. Changing the way you perceive pressure and focusing on the right things will reduce ironic processes and fewer mental resources will be taken up worrying about performance. However, there are some more specific ways you can combat ironic processes if you feel that your performance is particularly affected by it.

Empty your head

Instead of trying not to worry, or trying to suppress concerns about a match, it may be more beneficial to express these worries and concerns instead. Expressing your thoughts, instead of suppressing your thoughts, means that you are no longer expending mental resources trying to control your thoughts, so you therefore eliminate a key requirement for the production of ironic effects. What we often do with athletes is have them write down, on a sheet of paper, exactly what is on their mind regarding the upcoming important match. Then they read what they have written (one time only), before ripping the piece of paper up, and throwing it in the bin. Expressing worries and concerns in writing to oneself is an important step in conquering the occurrence of ironic processes.

Be ironic to fight irony

Ironic processes work so well because you try not to think about the thing you really don't want to happen. For example, you have an important match coming up but in your last performance you lost a wicket trying to play a regular defensive stroke to an average delivery. Going into this next match, you are plagued with thoughts of your failure in the last match days before your performance.

At this point, the trick is not to suppress these thoughts, but to let them flow into your head and play out unrestricted. However, there is one important rule you need to follow. It would be unwise to let unwanted thoughts run free on the day of your performance, or even the night before. What we would suggest is that you specifically make time in the days leading up to your performance to think about those past failures and let your mind drift back to the events. You may even think about the same thing happening in your next match. The trick is to think about the very thing you don't want to happen.

As you think about this unwanted experience, you may experience a couple of things. First, you may start to realise that, actually, it wasn't as bad as you first thought and that you were able to cope with the setback. As we suggested earlier, even your sporting heroes have failed, and you will have failed many times but have come back having been through tough times. Second, by thinking about the unwanted experience, that is, by exposing yourself to an outcome that you want to avoid, you may actually fear that outcome less. This is known as desensitisation and it simply means that because you are making yourself think about the thing you fear, you learn not to fear it. By accepting that failure happens and by allowing yourself to think about unwanted outcomes, you remove the need for thought suppression and therefore remove ironic processes.

Adapt

"There were plenty of times when I was out of my comfort zone when I was playing cricket... In fact, when I was playing in front of a full house at the MCG with thousands of Aussies having a go at me, I was as far as you can get from being comfortable." Andrew Flintoff

"You must practice your batting as if you are playing in a game... Put yourself under pressure to complete the goal you have set for yourself, whether it is seeing off the new ball or closing the game out under pressure... Create pressure and intensity when you train. One way is when you are having a net against bowlers, you bat against them till one of them gets you out. Once you are out, then that's the end of your net." Owais Shah

We have just talked about the idea of desensitisation to unwanted thoughts and fears as a way to fight ironic process, which leads nicely on to a similar and highly important strategy for thriving under pressure. The two quotes above from Andrew Flintoff and Owais Shah suggest that the way to adapt to pressure (or the way to thrive under pressure) is to experience pressure and get used to it. As Andrew

Flintoff suggests, there will be times when you feel out of your comfort zone when performing which, if you are not prepared, may interfere with your performance at crucial points.

Typically, those who struggle to cope with performance discomfort change their routines; they behave and think differently, and often seem like a different player out in the middle. This is sending the body and the brain a message: "*I am not comfortable, I am worried, I don't want to be here.*" Not the best way to approach a performance.

When you change the way you approach a match, you are likely to change the way you perform, usually for the worse. So, the quote from Owais Shah becomes very important indeed. By practicing under pressure, by making your training as realistically demanding as you can (setting tough targets), and by creating an intense environment (turn up the heating, imagine a huge crowd), you learn to cope with the pressure and get used to feeling uncomfortable in tough situations.

By putting the mind and body through pressure, you adapt to it, so in actual match situations you know how to focus your mind and realise that those physiological sensations you experience are normal and helpful. As you can imagine, this can give you great confidence because going into demanding match situations you can say: "*I've been here before, I know how to cope.*" To be clear, you don't need to create a situation comparable to the final of the Ashes (indeed creating this would be impossible). It is important to recognise that training, even under some pressure, can help inoculate you against future match pressure. So *seek pressure* in training and carry these experiences with you to actual matches. See *Chapter Five* on *Becoming Mentally Tough* in this book, also.

Bringing it all together

"*I am always fascinated to watch how a guy handles a pressure situation. Some players become animated, some train extra hard, some withdraw – but the true greats keep their self-belief, trust themselves and continue to work away, knowing that if the foundations have been established, good form will come.*" Steve Waugh in his 2005 Autobiography.

Chapter 4

Feeling challenged

In this chapter we have unpacked the notion of pressure and explained just how pressure can disrupt performance.

We talked about the mental implications of perceived pressure, discussing important mechanisms such as paralysis by analysis, ironic processes, and tunnel vision. We also talked about the physiological implications of perceived pressure, outlining that specific changes in our cardiovascular system, caused by our mental approach to demanding situations, can have a significant impact on our performance.

We then went on to propose a number of ways in which you can learn to deal with pressure, involving the development of new skills and ways of thinking to aid you in your quest to perform well when it really matters. The final part of this chapter will advocate the development of a 'Challenge Strategy' that encompasses most of the psychological strategies we have discussed in this chapter.

If you remember, a challenge state occurs when athletes have high self-confidence in their ability to perform well, perceive themselves to have great control over their skills and approach, and are focused on what they want to achieve (rather than focusing on avoiding failure). This psychological approach to demanding performance situations is linked to a more efficient physiological response, helpful for performance. So promoting these three psychological factors is highly important if you are to fulfil your potential under pressure.

Importantly, you should realise that these three psychological factors can be controlled *by you*. You can increase your self-confidence, perceptions of control, and can frame your goals in a way that you are striving to succeed, not trying to avoid failure.

Self-Confidence

One of the major sources of self-confidence is past success. When approaching important performance situations, think back to the times when you have performed well in similar circumstances. Use the ideas of training under pressure to create these successful experiences that you can use in your imagery to 'see' yourself coping and performing well under pressure. Focus on what you need to do to perform well and 'see' yourself coping and performing well in the upcoming match. See *Chapter Six* on *Playing Confidently* in this book for more ideas on how to increase this aspect.

Control

Focus only on what you can control (effort, positivity, intent) and only on the three things you need to do to perform well. Draw from previous experiences under pressure and realise that you have been there before and therefore you have control over the skills required to perform well. Also, realise that having a strategy in place to help you thrive under pressure has allowed you to control your mental preparation for performance; this can never be underestimated. Recognise that those physical symptoms of pressure you feel are normal and can help you to perform at your best.

Approach Focus

Regard the upcoming match as an opportunity to show how good you are and think of demanding situations as challenges to be overcome. Be positive in your approach. Instead of trying to avoid failure or thinking "*Don't mess up*", only fill your mind with the thoughts and images of you performing well. Recognise the importance of demanding situations, but be realistic and logical in how you frame your goals. Remember, *wanting* to succeed more than anything in the world is better than *demanding* that you must succeed.

Summary

Pressure is ubiquitous in cricket, you can't avoid it. As Imran Khan says: "*Cricket is a pressure game*", but this pressure is created by *you* in *your mind*, and therefore can be controlled by you. By having a more logical perspective on success and failure, and by reinforcing self-confidence, control, and approach goals, using the psychological skills discussed in this book, you can learn to thrive under pressure. Like James Anderson, you too can "*Thrive on pressure*", by mastering your psychological approach when it matters most.

Chapter 4

In the following chapter we explore the importance of mental toughness for cricket performance, and how you can increase your mental toughness for competition.

Key messages:

- Thinking too much about cricket performance (i.e., technique) can increase the likelihood of choking under pressure
- Avoid irony in your self-talk during cricket
- Focus on relevant pieces of information when performing (e.g., watch the ball)
- When faced with pressure situations individuals will either be challenged or threatened. Challenge states lead to better performance
- Thriving under pressure is about smart thinking, positive imagery, clear focus, and enjoying the challenge of competition

Further reading:

Beilock, S. (2011). *Choke: What the secrets of the brain reveal about getting it right when you have to*. Free Press, New York.

Advanced reading:

Jones, M., Meijen, C., McCarthy, P. J., & Sheffield, D. (2009). A theory of challenge and threat states in athletes. *International Review of Sport and Exercise Psychology, 2*, 161-180.

Jones, M. V., & Turner, M. J. (2012). In P, Totterdell, & K, Niven (Eds.), *Should I strap a battery to my head? (And other questions about emotion)*. Printed by Createspace.

Turner, M. J., Jones, M. V., Sheffield, D., & Cross, S. L. (2012). Cardiovascular indices of challenge and threat states predict performance under stress in cognitive and motor tasks. *International Journal of Psychophysiology, 86*, 48-57.

Wegner, D. M. (1989). *White bears and other unwanted thoughts: Suppression, obsession, and the psychology of mental control*. New York: Viking/Penguin.

5

Becoming Mentally Tough

"True colours are best displayed when facing adversity. Mental toughness is about never giving into yourself, never taking the easy option. Having a reputation for being mentally tough can have enormous advantages, because opponents respect and admire that trait and will put you on a bit of a pedestal." Steve Waugh

Cricket provides many illustrations of mental toughness. For example, consider Sir Ian Botham's performance at Headingley in 1981 against Australia. From a seemingly impossible match winning situation, Botham (with support from his teammates) scored a belligerent hundred under the upmost pressure which not only changed the outcome of the match in favour of England but also the course of the whole series.

Further, Shane Warne, regarded by many to be one of the finest bowlers of all time, took over 1000 international wickets in an international career spanning more than 15 years. However, alongside his successes, he had to deal with several career threatening injuries. Importantly, despite his injury issues, Warne continued to perform optimally at the highest levels on a consistent basis.

More recently, in the 2010-2011 Ashes, Alastair Cook scored 766 runs in 5 tests (including three hundreds and a top score of 235 not out) at an average of 127.66 to arguably lead England to their first series win in Australia since 1986. And even more recently, we have witnessed Michael Clarke achieve the phenomenal feat of becoming the first test player to score four double centuries in a calendar year.

Whilst these examples may imply that being successful is a sign of mental toughness, as we shall see in this chapter - mental toughness is typically about the attitudes, thoughts, and behaviours that individuals demonstrate when under pressure, dealing with adversity, and whilst staying committed and dedicated.

Essentially though, what do the above examples demonstrate about mental toughness in cricket? First, all of the performers arguably had an unshakable belief in their abilities during the specific situations they found themselves in (see *Chapter Six* on *Playing Confidently*).

Second, it is likely they all invested a large amount of effort (either mental or physical) in their preparation, their performances, or both.

Third, they all demonstrated excellent coping skills in dealing with the demands and adversity of high-level cricket performance, along with being able to deal with the many life stressors that can potentially affect professional sports people (e.g., dealing with the media, being away from home, a loss of form, injuries).

Finally, all of the players demonstrated a high level of resilience in being able to bounce-back and deal with setbacks and challenges.

There is a lot we can learn about becoming mentally tough from examples such as the ones presented earlier. However, one of the key questions we may ask at this juncture is where did they get their mental toughness from? Was it inherited or practiced? Essentially, are we born mentally tough or do we learn it through life experiences?

There is a wealth of theory and research from sport psychology that we can draw upon to help us understand mental toughness better, and learn how we might develop mental toughness ourselves or in the players we work with. In this chapter you will see some crossover with other chapters in this book. This is not done because we aim to repeat ourselves but moreover it is an illustration of the broad nature of the term mental toughness.

In this chapter we outline what mental toughness is and, specifically, what mental toughness is in cricket, before we outline a number of possible strategies to help foster mental toughness which players and coaches can draw upon.

What is Mental Toughness?

Mental toughness has been frequently associated with sporting success by athletes, coaches, and sport psychologists. The term was originally popularized by Jim Loehr, in the 1980s, who considered that at least 50% of superior athletic performance was attributable to mental factors.

Mental toughness has become a frequently used layman's term for athlete's tolerance to the demands of pressurized sport and optimal levels of performance. For example, mental toughness is often the all-encompassing term many coaches, spectators, and commentators use to describe the superior mental characteristics of successful elite cricketers.

Indeed, separating 'great' from 'good' players may be due to mental toughness when physical, technical, and tactical skills are equal. Typically, 'good' cricketers are those who make it to the elite level but do not achieve with the same consistency and magnitude that 'great' players with mental toughness do. It could therefore be argued that whilst unprecedented physical ability is needed to make it to an elite level, mental toughness may be the major distinction between 'good' and 'great' cricketers.

Research from sport psychology has predominantly focused on understanding the construct of mental toughness by interviewing elite athletes (e.g., Olympic gold medallists) deemed to be or have been 'mentally tough' and elite coaches who have worked alongside mentally tough athletes. Data have therefore indicated a number of characteristics ascribed to mental toughness in sport. These include:

- Self-belief
- Concentration and focus
- Motivation (including determination and commitment)
- Thriving on competition
- Resilience
- Handling pressure
- Positive attitude
- Quality preparation
- Perseverance

Therefore, in its broadest sense mental toughness is an umbrella term used by many involved in sport and cricket when referring to the difference between good and great cricketers. Table 5.1 presents a summary of the key characteristics that have emerged from research in sport psychology.

Given the broad nature of mental toughness (exemplified by the many characteristics outlined in Table 5.1), sport psychologists' understanding of mental toughness has also been hampered by the many definitions that have been produced. Therefore, in this chapter we draw upon the work of Daniel Gucciardi (a leading researcher on mental toughness in cricket) and define mental toughness in cricket as the following:

"...coping with the many demands (of cricket and life) and staying more consistent in remaining determined, focused, confident, and in control under pressure."

This definition encapsulates the main aspects of what it is to be mentally tough in cricket, but also helps players and coaches to understand areas they can work on to develop mental toughness (e.g., staying focused, dealing with pressure).

Table 5.1, Mental toughness characteristics in sport.

Mental Toughness Characteristics	*Example*
1. Having an unshakeable self-belief in your ability to achieve your competition goals.	*"If you want to be the best in the world you have to be strong enough to believe you are capable of that."*
2. Bouncing back from performance setbacks as a result of increased determination to succeed.	*"Yeah, we all have them (setbacks), the mentally tough performer doesn't let them affect him, he uses them."*
3. Having an unshakable self-belief that you possess unique qualities and abilities that make you better than your opponents.	*"He made the right decisions about how he was going to train, but he had the self-belief in his ability to know that he was making the right decisions."*

4. Having an insatiable desire, and internalized motives to succeed.	*"Will do almost anything (within the rules) to succeed whatever the cost (e.g., win)."*
5. Remaining fully focused on the task at hand in the face of competition-specific distractions.	*"If you want to be the best, you have to be totally focused on what you are doing."*
6. Regaining psychological control following unexpected, uncontrollable events (competition-specific).	*"Even when you think things are against you, like abandoned matches, the weather...the mentally tough performer is able to compose himself and come back and still win."*
7. Pushing back the boundaries of physical and emotional pain, while still maintaining technique and effort under distress (in training and competition).	*"It is a question of pushing yourself...it's mind over matter, just trying to hold your technique and performing while under this distress and going beyond your limits."*
8. Accepting that competition anxiety is inevitable and knowing that you can cope with it.	*"I accept that I'm going to get nervous, particularly when the pressure's on, but keeping the lid on it and being in control is crucial."*
9. Thriving on the pressure of competition.	*"Mental toughness is being resilient and using competition pressure to get the best out of yourself."*
10. Not being adversely affected by others' good and bad performances.	*"The mentally tough performer uses others good performances as a spur rather than saying 'I can't go that fast'. They say 'well, he is no better than me,' so I'm going to go out there and beat him."*

11. Remaining fully-focused in the face of personal life distractions.	*"Once you're in the competition, you cannot let you mind wander to other things…It doesn't matter what has happened to you, you can't bring the problem into the performance arena."*
12. Switching a sport focus on and off as required.	*"You need to be able to switch it (i.e., focus) on and off, especially between games during a tournament. The mentally tough performer succeeds by having control of the on/off switch."*

Mental Toughness in Cricket

Given the importance that players, coaches, and psychologists have attached to mental toughness, investigations have taken place in cricket to more eloquently outline where mental toughness comes from, and how it can be developed.

One key piece of research during recent years has been compiled by sport psychologists working with the England and Wales Cricket Board (ECB; Bull, Shambrook, James, & Brooks, 2005). They conducted extensive interviews with 12 English cricketers identified as being among the most mentally tough players during the previous 20 years. Essentially, data from the interviews yielded important and interesting information about how these players had become mentally tough.

Importantly, the research identified that mental toughness is a notion that can be developed and is not necessarily something which is inherited. The ECB research identified the role of a *cricketer's environment* influencing 'Tough Character', 'Tough Attitudes', and 'Tough Thinking' and a mental toughness pyramid or framework was formed to understand the development of mental toughness in elite English cricketers. Figure 5.1 provides an illustration of this model. The following sections provide a synthesis of this ECB research using quotes from the interviewed players.

Figure 5.1, The Mental Toughness Pyramid. Adapted from Bull et al. (2005).

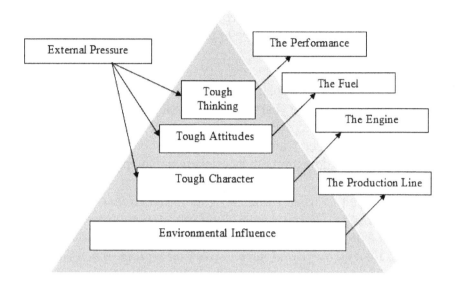

'Environmental influence' underpins the whole framework and is considered the production line for developing mental toughness. In turn, it is suggested to be the most important area upon which to focus resources and to illustrate this further, data from the interviews revealed four areas of importance. First, that for all of the players, one or both parents were an important influence at various stages in their upbringing in relation to the development of mental toughness in cricket.

"Obviously my father has been a huge influence. He pushed me immensely and ruled with the stick a little, but would make sure I did it well. He would have the most mental influence on me in 90% a good way...every innings was important, it wasn't just 'that's another game of cricket'...He was the one that always pushed me and backed me and did everything."

Second, exposure to foreign cricket was also reported to be a key environmental influence. To this end, those players who had travelled to, and played cricket, in Australia and South Africa indicated how important that experience was to them. Fundamentally it appeared that such situations provided players with a sense of being an 'outsider' at a new club which, in turn, developed a hardened mind-set and approach to cricket. For example, one player commented:

"I went to a cricket club where people didn't know who I was and, being an Englishman in Australia, you're always going to be looked to, not so much down on, but you have to prove yourself more than an Australian."

Third, data highlighted that players had not always been successful throughout their formative years of playing cricket and thus had experienced and survived early career setbacks. Moreover, players reported that they valued 'failures' and viewed them as positive experiences in their development as cricketers. One player commented:

"I must have been 15 when I was going to be signed up as a leg spinner and then just lost it. That was mentally a very defining year for me. You've gone from being a hero in your school to being a bloke who's lost it... To then go away and have to work on batting. When you're 15 trying to work out whether you want to do it anymore."

Finally in relation to environmental influence, data also revealed a players' perception that hard work had helped to fuel their ambition to be successful. Further, once the players knew what had to be achieved to earn success in cricket - this knowledge then served as motivation to help them maintain their levels of success.

In the pyramid (as outlined in Figure 5.1) the environment is suggested to set the base upon which 'Tough Character' is developed. Tough character is posited to be the engine room for players' mental toughness. Data from the interviews on this aspect again highlighted a number of key findings, particularly in relation to crucial personality characteristics relative to mental toughness.

First, the players demonstrated an ability to be independent and to take responsibility for themselves, in relation to their professional development within cricket and in their general life. One player noted:

"What you need to do is go to Perth or Sydney, anywhere you're on your own with no Mum or Dad to look after you. You've got to look after yourself, you've got to present yourself to the team you play for and show them what you can do. You're either sink or swim. You'll get

up and mature, stand up for yourself, think things out for yourself and work things out on your own."

Second, it was very clear that the elite players had very good self-reflection skills and that self-reflection had taken place throughout their careers. This skill had accordingly impacted on their ability to maintain high standards, confidence, and performances. The importance of self-reflection is outlined in the following quote:

"I'm not the most gifted batsman but I can make up for that by using my brain. I have to be very aware of what I am doing –what I can, and cannot do, in any particular situation."

Third, the players clearly had a strong desire to be the best cricketers they could be, but also be the best players they could be relative to their own potential. To illustrate, one player noted:

"I want to play against the best bowlers - I want to play against the best. That's the challenge for me."

Finally and to some extent most importantly, the players reported an unshakeable (or robust) self-belief in their ability to be successful cricketers (see also *Chapter Six* on *Playing Confidently*). A resilient level of confidence was also highlighted in the following quote from one of the players:

"It's something that's been there all the way. I suppose in a way it's having an inner confidence that if you wanted to, you could beat him, and you're not worried about losing to him every now and then. I had seventeen dropped catches in the series, which is enough to finish a lot of people off, and I still finished leading wicket taker with 21 wickets. The biggest thing for me is self-belief, that's all, because…whatever it was instilled into me…if you don't believe in yourself, then why should anyone else?"

Tough character is considered to be fairly stable and generalizable across different situations and is a precursor to the development of 'Tough Attitudes'. In the pyramid this is referred to as a player's mental toughness fuel from which they draw upon.

Chapter 5

The interviews yielded further information about a number of key mental toughness attitudes the players had. These attitudes included:

- An ability to exploit learning opportunities (i.e., a desire to use learning opportunities to keep learning, and to learn from failure)
- A belief in quality preparation (i.e., quality and consistent practice and preparation)
- Use of self-set challenging targets (i.e., being competitive with oneself and setting challenging performance targets)
- A *"Never say die"* mindset (e.g., producing performances when it was essential to do so)
- A determination to make the most of their ability (i.e., not necessarily being the most naturally gifted players, but having an unshakeable desire to succeed)
- A belief in making a difference (i.e., a belief that they alone could be the person in the team who could make a difference)

Further, players had a *"go the extra mile"* mindset demonstrating an ability to repeatedly work harder to get the most out of their abilities. To illustrate, one player commented:

"It's who wants it the most. Who is the most committed? Who is the one prepared to go that little bit extra to get more out themselves in whatever sphere necessary. I'm only gonna achieve that through my own hard work, and you've got to back that up by being prepared to put in the hard work."

Players also outlined that they thrived on competition and the pressure to perform, whilst maintaining a clear attitude towards approaching matches, with one player revealing:

"That's the winning moment, I mean you can't beat that moment and that's where everything, what you've achieved, all you've done, comes out and there's no stopping that. That's not an act - that's just everything. The pressure. Everything that's built up-and then you just let it go. And that's why I play. You can't beat that moment."

Finally, it was evident from the players that most had, at some point, taken calculated career risks to help them develop and attain their goals. The following quote provides an illustration of a player willing to take risks to advance his career:

"I was completely out of the England frame for lack of form. I had to sit down with my wife and say 'look I've got these two options. I could either not do anything this winter - just get a job and do well for my county - but I need to get back in the England side and if I'm going to do that I need to go away. I'm going to have to leave you for six months, go away and just work hard at everything'. So I went off to abroad and the next year I got 1,500 runs and was back in and captain of the A tour."

Finally, 'Tough Thinking' forms the top of the pyramid and represents the key mental qualities of being 'mentally tough' in actual performance situations (i.e., the performance aspect). This aspect relates directly to the important thought patterns a player should have in relation to being successful in cricket.

In essence, these thought patterns relate to a player's level of self-awareness (see *Chapter Seven* on *Controlling Your Emotions*), robust self-confidence (see *Chapter Six* on *Playing Confidently*) and the ability to think clearly.

In relation to robust self-confidence it was revealed that an ability to make use of robust confidence during matches was influenced by three areas:

1. Overcoming self-doubts (e.g., an unshakeable belief that you are able to perform at the highest level)
2. Feeding off one's physical condition (i.e., confidence was enhanced knowing that your body was in robust physical condition and not prone to weakness)
3. Maintaining self-focus (i.e., focusing on personal needs to maintain performance)

The 'thinking clearly' attribute highlighted that players were aware of their thoughts, understood what they needed to think and focus on at a given time during matches, and were able to maintain control of their thinking (see also *Chapter Four* on *Performing Under Pressure*). Indeed, thinking clearly in cricket was influenced by:

- Good decision-making (i.e., being able to make the right decisions with confidence and commitment under extreme pressure)
- Keeping perspective (e.g., cricket is only a game at the end of the day)
- Honest self-appraisal (e.g., knowing strengths and limitations and making performance decisions accordingly)

In summary, this research reveals a fascinating look into the key mental qualities of some of English cricket's most mentally tough players. In addition, it also offers insight into some of the ways mental toughness can be developed and maintained. Before we move into key strategies and practices, we explore how players and coaches can measure mental toughness.

Measuring Mental Toughness in Cricket

Recently, the ECB has developed the Mental Toughness Profiler (MTP) as a mechanism with which to help cricketers, coaches and support staff develop performance.

The MTP includes four dimensions of mental toughness in cricket:

1. Fight
2. Inner Drive
3. Critical Moment Control
4. Resilience

The MTP is completed via discussions between a sport psychologist and coach about an individual cricketer. Ratings are given on each of the four mental toughness dimensions. The results are used to provide player feedback, identify developmental training interventions, and to inform the selection process for national squads.

More recently a specific measure of mental toughness in cricket has been developed by sport psychologists working with Cricket Australia (CA). The Cricket Mental Toughness Inventory (CMTI) is a 15-item measure that assesses five key facets of cricket mental toughness:

1. Emotional intelligence
2. Desire to achieve
3. Resilience
4. Concentration control
5. Self-belief

The CMTI provides coaches, players, and sport psychologists with a mechanism to determine mental toughness levels across time, to explore changes that may require intervention.

The current drive to produce valid and reliable measures is welcomed and should play a role in helping coaches and sport psychologists determine players' levels of mental toughness. On a cautionary note, a level of scepticism should be maintained regarding the use of mental toughness measures as a means for selecting players. In essence, such measures currently lack sufficient predictive validity and are prone to response bias by players. In summary, we would recommend using mental toughness measures to increase awareness of players' mental toughness and determine if, and when, intervention is required.

Developing and Maintaining Mental Toughness

Because mental toughness is perceived to help develop over a player's career, it makes sense, therefore, for players to receive support and specific mental toughness training from an early age rather than in the later stages of their careers (unless appropriate). Based upon on mental toughness research (i.e., ECB research) in sport psychology, and our own experiences of working in elite cricket, in this section we outline a number of strategies and activities with which players and coaches can maximize mental toughness.

Self-Confidence for Mental Toughness

One of the recurring themes to be derived from our understanding of mental toughness is that mentally tough players are typically very self-confident and have an unshakeable self-belief in their abilities. It is not within the scope of this chapter to go into specific detail about where players derive self-confidence from, and how it can be enhanced (see *Chapter Six* on *Playing Confidently* for more specific information).

However, it is important to note that players should be encouraged to learn to develop an awareness of the effects of confidence on performance, along with the sources from which they derive their confidence (e.g., preparation, coaches, video analysis).

Arguably, the more self-confident a player is, the more mentally tough they are. Self-confident players look forward to the pressure of competition, never give in, work hard, think that they can make a difference, and take calculated risks which can be the difference between winning and losing. Therefore, time and work on enhancing players' self-confidence may also prove beneficial in the development of mental toughness beliefs and attitudes. We encourage this type of activity to commence early on in a player's career given the importance of self-confidence on cricket performance but also the importance relative to fostering mental toughness.

Coping with Adversity

The importance of coping with adversity has been identified as a key factor in mental-toughness. Adversity in cricket is likely to relate to a loss of form, recovering from an injury, and being de-selected.

In cricket, players will use both *approach* and *avoidance* coping styles - the former involving a player dealing with a stressor (e.g., a loss of form) by engaging with it, and the latter by dismissing it as unimportant.

In essence, players will see adversity situations as either a challenge or a threat and that perception will impact upon whether they approach the situation (i.e., challenge perception) or avoid it (i.e., threat perception; see also *Chapter Four* on *Performing Under Pressure*).

Typically, mentally tough players will use more approach coping strategies and less avoidance strategies. Avoidance-focused coping strategies, as the name suggests, include:

- Avoidance (e.g., faking injury, making excuses)
- Detachment
- Denial, and wishful thinking
- Ignoring or blocking things out

- Self-blame

Examples of successful approach strategies identified include constructive evaluation, positive images, concentration control, keeping sight of the whole picture, and positive thinking.

It is, of course, important for players to learn techniques to help in dealing with failure or setbacks (i.e., adversity). One technique that can be effective in this regard is positive reappraisal (i.e., evaluating a setback in a positive manner). Underlying this process we posit that a failure or setback situation generates a player's self-talk which can be either positive or negative. Positive self-talk tends to be specific and temporary (e.g., "*I didn't bat well today, but I can work hard this week in practice, and my next innings will be different*"). However, if self-talk is negative it is loaded with permanent, pervasive, and personal information (i.e., "*I am not a good player against spin and cannot ever see myself doing well in the subcontinent on turning pitches*").

Whichever type of explanations are used to explain failure they lead to changes in a player's emotions (e.g., positive or negative). For example, positive self-talk leads to positive emotions and underlying hopefulness that leads to determination, self-confidence, motivation and persistence. Conversely, negative self-talk leads to negative emotions including hopelessness, inadequacy, powerlessness, and low motivation.

If a player demonstrates negative self-talk about adverse situations they should be encouraged to transform the negative evaluations, and associated self-talk, with more positive, specific, and temporary self-talk that offers counter-arguments to the negative self-talk thereby replacing the negative feelings with more positive and productive ones (see the self-talk exercise in the *Playing Confidently Chapter*).

In addition to reappraisal, a number of alternative mental skills can be used with players to encourage successful coping; these include:

- Reflection on positive past performances (see *Chapter Three* on *Staying Focused*)
- Pre-performance routines (see *Chapter Three* on *Staying Focused*)

- Relaxation techniques (see *Chapter Seven* on *Controlling Your Emotions*)

Practice as you Compete

One of the key differences we often observe is that players and teams typically practice very differently in comparison to how they compete. This undoubtedly means that players will find it hard to perform when faced with challenging and pressurized situations. For example, prior to an important T20 game some players and teams will prepare by hitting full-tosses as far as they can with no consequence for poor performance (completely the opposite to a game situation).

From our experiences it is typical that practice can sometimes be somewhat relaxed, and easy paced, and thus lack the intensity which game situations bring. Ideally, players should practice hard and play easy. But what does this imply? Our understanding of this adage is that players need to experience *pressure, consequences*, and to some extent *failure* in practice to develop and maintain mental toughness. In the following section we outline a couple of ways for the practice hard and play easy adage to become reality.

Pressure Testing

In our work with academy and professional players we structure their training schedules with pressure testing opportunities on key cricket skills (e.g., batting, bowling, and fielding). For example, in our fielding test, players are informed that they are required to successfully complete a minimum of 28 from 30 random catches using a bowling machine. In addition, they are informed that they are in competition with each other and that their scores will be posted for all to see (ego threatening instructions). The premise of these tests is to regularly expose players to pressure so that they become desensitized (i.e., used to pressure) and thus are more able to deal with it during games.

The desensitization premise is very much influenced by what we know from other disciplines including the military. To illustrate, new recruits are often exposed to the crackle and noise of gunfire and explosions (in controlled situations) from very early on in their training so that they become used to such situations. Ultimately, these situations are created to reduce the likelihood of individuals choking under pressure when they eventually go into combat or the test arena (see *Chapter Four: Performing Under Pressure* for more information).

Consequence Training and Burning-Bridges Training

In many ways that are similar to pressure testing, consequence training is about creating practice and training situations which have a perceived level of importance by players. As we mentioned earlier, training can sometimes be relaxed and different to games, therefore what we try to do in consequence training is to increase the intensity, and to some extent the pressure, on players.

Typical consequence training has required players (on regular occasions) to deliver a specified level of performance (e.g., survive a short pitch bowling session, score 90% success rate on a catching test). When the specified targets are not attained, players are presented with a series of consequences, including missing future sessions, doing extra fitness sessions, and doing chores (e.g., washing dinner plates, clothes) for other teammates.

Consequence training is about developing a perception in players that success is earned and not something that happens, along with creating positive beliefs and expectations about wanting to perform and thrive under pressure.

Aligned with consequence training is that of *burning-bridge training*. Here players undertake tasks which (unbeknown to them at the start) cannot be achieved. Indeed, the tasks are typically too difficult for their skill level or impossible to achieve. In these situations we are interested in assessing the behavioural responses players demonstrate (e.g., maintained or withdrawn effort and persistence).

To this end, we can learn a lot about the mental toughness of players, given that mentally tough individuals (it is suggested) keep going when the impossible is still perceived as possible. These burning-bridge situations provide players with feelings of failure or a setback which, as noted earlier, is suggested to enhance mental toughness. Additionally, players can reflect on the lessons learned from such situations and therefore increase their self-awareness about how they would approach similar situations in the future.

Whilst regular pressure testing and consequence training has an important role to play in the development of players' mental toughness, coaches and sport psychologists should counsel players carefully so they are clear about the aims and the importance of meeting performance standards.

Mastering Failure

Ultimately, in our work we try to encourage our players to master failure - that is how to handle it and how to learn from it.

Culturally, failure is not something that is openly encouraged, particularly in academic and sporting contexts, by teachers and coaches. However, there are many illustrations of individuals who learn from failure. For example, consider the meltdown of the golfer Rory McIlroy at the US Masters in 2011. During the final round, after being in a seemingly unassailable lead, McIlroy faltered and carded an 80 leaving him tied for 15th place. Following such a failure it would, of course, be easy for most players to question their ability as a golfer and perhaps want to avoid future pressurized situations. Interestingly, though, McIlroy's meltdown appeared to motivate him and he bounced back more determined than ever to win his first golf major. Two months later he won that first major at the US Open, breaking several landmark records on the way. Arguably, this is an illustration of an athlete who had mastered failure.

One of the big issues we encounter in our work with cricketers is a fear of failure, a fear of underperforming, a fear of letting others and themselves down. Typically, this fear exists because they have actually never really failed.

The longer players go without failure, the more it looms large over their heads. The evidence we identified early on illustrates that *failure is useful* for players in developing mental toughness, but probably because it allows a philosophy to develop around failure being a naturally occurring phenomenon and something which happens to everyone.

One useful exercise is to get players to consider a role model, a star, a hero they have, and ask them if that person has ever failed. In all situations, they will have failed and probably on more than one occasion. This exercise demonstrates that humans are fallible and prone to mistakes and failure, and these events offer a potentially liberating perspective about failure for players and coaches alike (see also *Chapter Four* on *Performing Under Pressure* for more information on smart thinking).

Encouraging players to not make mistakes arguably interferes with the learning process, but also violates a number of assumptions about top level performance.

1. A fear of making mistakes encourages players to be tentative and tense and hampers them from staying relaxed and taking calculated risks.
2. It encourages choking under pressure because players are so concerned about the negative consequence they forget about the things that will help them to play well.
3. Fear of failure can reduce a player's level of commitment and enjoyment of cricket - leaving them demotivated and disinterested.

Overall, teaching players that mistakes and failing is part of the process, encourages them to play with freedom, enjoyment, confidence, and commitment.

Exposing Players to Foreign Conditions

One important finding from the research on English cricketers is that most had experienced playing cricket in foreign conditions, and these experiences not only enhanced their cricket mental toughness, but had also had important consequences in terms of developing independence and robust confidence.

From our experience of cricket in England, many counties now encourage their players from academy through to senior levels to play in foreign conditions at regular intervals. To illustrate, some of the academies that we work with schedule regular training and playing tours, where players are exposed to foreign cultures, climates, playing conditions, and opponents. Indeed, trips to India bring a very different challenge for players than trips to Australia given the marked differences in playing conditions and opponents' techniques.

In addition, many professional players whom we work with are encouraged to head off to play cricket in foreign conditions during the off-season to enable them to get playing time and to develop themselves as people. To this end, players learn a lot about themselves and their games when they independently travel to a new country to become the overseas professional for a new team. At an international level the ECB also sends many players to different countries throughout the winter for technique, conditioning, and mental toughness development (e.g., fast bowling program in South Africa, spin bowling camp in India).

In summary, we recognize that sending players and teams to different countries is likely to be costly and logistically prohibitive. However, where possible, we wholeheartedly support players and teams in wanting to experience playing in foreign conditions to enhance their mental toughness. From our experience it is important to ensure that players have appropriate support mechanisms in place when going away - to help them deal with challenging situations (e.g., homesickness, and a loss of form).

Team Building

In October 2010, the England cricket team spent five days in Nuremburg, Germany, sleeping in tents and engaging in a series of tasks including: abseiling, boxing, bungee jumps, and delivering personal speeches around a campfire to help them prepare mentally for the up and coming Ashes series. The stay included a trip to the war memorial site at Dachau. It was the first of Hitler's concentration camps, where more than 40,000 people died between 1933 and 1945. Andrew Strauss, the England captain at the time, commented:

"Following our trip to Flanders (First World War battlefields) last year, this was an opportunity for the players to spend time away from the cricketing environment, learn more about the wider world and develop ourselves both individually and collectively. It was a tough but rewarding five days and I know every player has gained greater insight

into themselves, their own team environment and environments outside cricket."

In sport there are many illustrations of teams going away to develop team building. Importantly, the above example illustrates that England players were destabilized (taken out of their comfort zones) in an attempt to develop their collective belief in dealing with challenges and adversity and ultimately their mental toughness. In addition, taking them to visit war memorials illustrates how the coaching staff were trying to develop philosophies that the sacrifices players have to make to play cricket, and the demands placed upon them, are nothing in comparison to what people who endured the concentration camps went through. Moreover, such situations bring a level of realism about playing cricket and that some things in life are more important.

Summary

Mental toughness is an umbrella term used by many cricket commentators, coaches, and players to explain how psychology affects performance at the highest level. Mentally tough cricketers have robust confidence, high levels of motivation, a desire to be successful, will to win, and have experienced failure or setbacks in their career.

The research findings from cricket are helpful and stimulating in that we now know about the contributing factors and strategies towards understanding and developing mental toughness. In this chapter we have outlined a number of contemporary techniques that we consider to be the most effective in increasing mental toughness in cricketers. In the following chapter we explore playing confidently in cricket and outline where cricket confidence comes from, and how we can maximize confidence at individual and team levels.

Key messages:

- Mental toughness is an essential feature for the development of excellence in cricket
- Mental toughness in cricket is: *"...coping with the many demands (of cricket and life) and staying more consistent in remaining determined, focused, confident, and in control under pressure."*

- Mental toughness in cricket is influenced by the environment, tough character, tough attitudes, and tough thinking
- Mental toughness in cricket can be developed and maintained by developing robust self-confidence, practicing under pressure, mastering failure, playing in challenging (foreign) conditions, and effective team building

Further reading:

Goldberg, A. S. (1998). *Sports slump busting: 10 steps to mental toughness and peak performance.* Champaign, IL: Human Kinetics.

Gucciardi, D. F., & Gordon, S. (2011). *Mental toughness in sport: Developments in theory and research.* Oxon: Routledge.

Jones, G., & Moorhouse, A. (2007). *Developing mental toughness.* Oxford: Springer Hill.

Advanced reading:

Bull, S., James, W., & Brooks, J. (2008). The Mental Toughness Profiler (MTP) for cricket. *On the Up*: *English Cricket Board (ECB) Coach Education*, August, 34-36.

Bull, S., Shambrook, C., James, W., & Brooks, J. (2005). Towards an understanding of mental toughness in elite English cricketers. *Journal of Applied Sport Psychology, 17,* 209-227.

Conaughton, D., Wadey, R., Hanton, S., & Jones, G. (2008). The development and maintenance of mental toughness: perceptions of elite performers. *Journal of Sport Sciences, 26,* 83-95.

Gucciardi, D. F., & Gordon, S. (2009). Development and preliminary validation of the Cricket Mental Toughness Inventory. *Journal of Sport Sciences, 27,* 1293-1310.

6

Playing Confidently

"When you have it (confidence) you feel like you're never going to lose it, when you haven't got it, you feel like you're never going to get it." Matthew Hayden

"The person who will whip me will be fast, strong, and hasn't even been born yet." Mohammed Ali

"When confidence is undermined, a player's whole game can be shot to pieces." Graham Gooch

If confidence could be packed into a pill it would be the most widely prescribed psychological pill on the market. For a moment, pause and reflect on your cricketing experiences. Think about when you were in control and bursting with confidence and think about when you were not. How did it feel? What happened to performance? Perhaps note this down.

Typically, when we are confident we feel in complete control of our skills, things happen as we expect, we approach situations as a challenge, and performance standards are high. Of course, when we have no confidence things are a struggle, our skills don't work, performance is poor, we start to question our abilities, and we avoid situations where we are put under pressure.

Most, if not all, cricketers and coaches appreciate the importance and benefits of high levels of self-confidence. In turn, most acknowledge that at varying points throughout a season and a career, players' and teams' confidence levels will fluctuate from high to low and have a significant effect on performance accordingly.

You don't need to be a very confident person socially to be a confident cricketer. Indeed there are many examples of relatively quiet and shy players who are transformed into very confident and vocal players on the pitch. If you are not a confident person there is no need to worry, it is what you think with the bat or ball in your hand that is important. Successful players back themselves. Believing that you can execute your skills correctly in any given situation, feeling you can win the duel (between bat and ball), and that your team can beat the opposition is vital.

Research in sport psychology clearly and consistently demonstrates self- and team confidence to be one of the most important psychological factors relative to sport performance. Indeed, higher levels of confidence encourage sport performers and teams to cope with, and enjoy, playing under pressure, as well as offering the freedom to express their abilities and talents, elevated motivation, and of course increased performance. In addition, with increased confidence, individuals and teams work harder (increased effort), are persistent in their skills and tasks, and set challenging goals - all of which are likely to contribute to increased performance.

In this chapter we will provide you with detail on confidence from both individual and team perspectives. Moreover, we will outline where confidence comes from, and by drawing on our own experiences and contemporary research, discuss a range of techniques that can be used to develop and maintain the confidence of players and teams alike.

What is Self-Confidence?

Self-confidence is the degree of certainty that you have in your ability to perform in a certain situation. So, for a cricketer, it is the degree of certainty you have in your ability to bat or bowl, catch or field.

Self-confidence is situation specific and we develop expectations about our ability to be successful in various situations. For example, one may have confidence about opening the batting against pace bowlers, but lower confidence when facing spin bowlers.

Confidence is interesting because it varies between individuals (e.g., Kevin Pietersen versus a club cricketer, facing a bowling machine set at 85mph), and within individuals (e.g., you could be very confident on one day in a given situation, and then not at all confident on the next day). Changes in your level of confidence influence the choices that you make, the execution of your skills, and how you evaluate your performance.

High levels of confidence are often misinterpreted as arrogance and complacency. However, this could not be further from the truth as confidence and arrogance are at two ends of a continuum. To illustrate, at one end we have a cricketer with high confidence, who works hard, is very persistent, and sets realistic yet challenging targets for themselves. At the other end, we have the arrogant cricketer, who may think they are too good to practice and train and hence reduces their effort levels, gives up easily when trying to develop their skills, and sets moderate training and performance goals - all of which lead to moderate levels of performance.

The quest for any serious cricketer is to have good levels of confidence, but more than this, the key is to have *consistent confidence* (regardless of whether you are playing well or poorly).

Even when playing poorly, if you are still confident you are more likely to play well again sooner than if you are playing poorly and lose your confidence. Indeed, contemporary research in sport psychology has begun to explore athletes' stability or 'robustness' of confidence. That is, the maintenance of levels of confidence when times are tough and obstacles are put in their paths. To illustrate, a cricketer with robust self-confidence is the player that bags two ducks in successive innings but is still training just as hard (if not harder) at the next training session.

Aligned with self-confidence is your attitude. Your attitude is your outlook on life, which then determines how you apply yourself in different situations. Coaches often talk about wanting players who have 'the right attitude', but what does this actually mean?

In the main, coaches are looking for positive (or optimistic) players who are hardworking. The second part of this is important. All of us have either a fixed or a growth mindset. A cricketer with a fixed mindset very much believes that you are born with what you have (i.e., you are either born naturally talented or not). If you are born good enough then great, any situation is a chance just to reinforce how good you are. Alternatively, if the fixed mindset players are not doing too well, they resort to excuses to explain poor performance and to justify why they, as good players, are not doing so well. This sort of player views failure as a judgement of their innate potential, and is reluctant to push themselves all the way to protect their self-esteem. The opposite (and advocated) mentality is a growth mindset. This approach views success as a result of hard work. Yes, some people are born more talented, but it is hard work that is important. A growth mindset says that whoever you are (e.g., a club player or the number one player in the world) you can always get better. As a result you will always seek to push yourself, relish hard work, and learn from mistakes. In this sense your attitude will underpin the type of person you are but also how hard you will work. We are all different (which is a good thing), but when it comes to cricket the more positive and growth-focused players we have in the team the better.

What is Team Confidence?

Similar to self-confidence, in many respects, is team confidence. In essence, team confidence is about the 'collective' belief in a team's ability to do well in given situations (e.g., a match against a top of the league team). Therefore, when teams go into certain situations (e.g., league games, or cup knock-outs) collectively the team will generate an expectation about whether they can be successful or not.

Think about whom you regard as the great cricket teams of the past and present. Typically they will have a firm understanding of one another, together with high levels of trust in their teammates' skills. Teams who have a positive expectation (i.e., are optimistic) about doing well are more likely to perform better than those teams who have a more negative expectation (i.e., they do not think they can achieve, or believe the opposition are better than they are).

Such expectations will, to some extent, be based on the experience of the group; past performances, the amount of positive communication amongst players and coaches, and the general 'mood' or 'emotions' of the group. The notion of emotional contagion can be particularly important in terms of teams' confidence. For example, if coaches and senior players in a dressing room appear to be tense and anxious prior to an important match or innings, it is likely the other players will pick up on these behaviours and begin to experience similar emotions.

In the same way that self-confidence has a number of benefits to performance, so too does team confidence. For example, teams with high levels of confidence always work hard and are persistent in trying to reach their goals. Consider the soccer team Manchester United. Many people consider their ability to score late goals a by-product of luck, or fortune; however the trend of scoring late goals happens too consistently for it to be luck. Indeed, what Manchester United demonstrates is a high level of team confidence. That is, they believe in their ability as a team to be successful in (most) situations. Accordingly, they are committed until the very end of matches (invest high levels of effort and concentration), keep persevering with skills, and make the right decisions. In contrast, teams with low confidence typically withdraw effort when competition becomes difficult or challenging, do not express themselves, and do not believe the impossible is possible.

Where does Confidence come from?

The psychologist Albert Bandura is rightly considered the leading authority on self-confidence related topics. The development of his theory of self-confidence in 1977 allowed him to be regarded by many as one of the most influential psychologists of the 20th century.

Bandura's theory proposed that self- and team confidence expectations are influenced by a number of sources of information which are drawn upon when forming an expectation about how well we think we can do in a given situation. These expectations will then have a direct influence on the behaviour (e.g., increased effort) and thought patterns (e.g., concerns and worries) of individuals and teams.

Figure 6.1 illustrates an adapted version of Bandura's (1997) model of self- and team confidence. The sources of information include past experiences, observation experiences, verbal instruction, physiological states, emotional states, and imaginal states.

Chapter 6

Figure 6.1, Sources of Self- and Team Confidence Information.
Adapted from Bandura (1997).

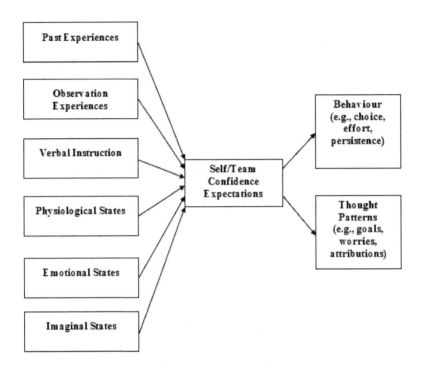

Past experience(s) are suggested to be the most influential source of confidence information because ultimately they are based on players' and teams' mastery experiences (i.e., success or failure in sporting situations). For example, if a cricketer repeatedly views past experiences as successes, self-confidence will be high. Conversely, if these experiences are viewed as failures, self-confidence will be low. Successful past performance experiences on difficult tasks (e.g., bowling well in batsman friendly conditions), without little external assistance (e.g., with fair umpiring decisions), together with occasional failures carry positive confidence information. In contrast situations that are easily attained with external help or tasks that are performed repeatedly with failure and hence indicate little progress carry limited confidence building information.

Past cricketing experiences can be built up over a long period of time (e.g., career averages and statistics to date), or over a shorter period of time (e.g., performance in the last few innings/games). Unfortunately though, if these are your only sources of confidence you are in trouble.

Experience works well when you are playing well (lots of runs or wickets, and great averages), but when you are not scoring runs or taking wickets you will lack confidence - not least because how confident you are can be dependent on other factors. You could have faced a couple of great balls, or the conditions may have been very favourable for the opposition. Either way, if you depend on form and stats you won't be in total control of your confidence. Therefore it is important to have an understanding of the other sources that players and teams can draw upon to enhance their confidence.

Confidence can also be derived through observing the performance of other players and noting the consequence of their performances. For example, an academy wicket keeper seeing a fellow wicket keeper of a similar level perform a difficult training routine successfully will increase levels of confidence (*"If they can do it then so can I"*). Observing peers in this way is suggested to present confidence information. To illustrate, observing repeated demonstrations by skilled cricketers can provide information to others on how to perform as well as confidence information that the task can be learnt and is attainable. For example, most cricketers will be able to relate to a situation when waiting to bat with the opposition dismissing your teammates' one after the other, in quick succession. As a result, in this particular situation you have limited successful observations to draw confidence from and may feel lower levels of confidence than normal when waiting to bat.

Verbal instruction can be provided by coaches, support staff, peers, parents, and by players themselves. For example, before a difficult task (e.g., batting for an hour before the close of play) a batsman may repeatedly tell themselves that they can succeed (see later in the chapter for information on *self-talk*). Indeed, this type of internal verbal instruction, and conversation provided externally by coaches and peers, can motivate players to persist in their efforts and serve to focus one's thoughts.

The capacity of this type of information to influence confidence depends on the prestige, credibility, expertise, and trustworthiness of the person(s) providing the instruction.

Whilst the message of providing confidence building information to oneself and to players is evident, the reality is somewhat different. More often than not the 'banter' in a dressing room can be to mock individuals about mistakes made in past performances rather than to build confidence. In addition, players will often use ironic self-talk about upcoming performance (e.g., "*Don't get out*"; see also the *Chapter: Performing Under Pressure*). Accordingly, it makes sense for teams and individuals to consider the type of verbal information they present - to try and maximize confidence. External verbal instruction may also be subliminally presented to players whilst in the dressing room through the use of mottos or slogans that encapsulate confident behaviours (e.g., train hard, play easy, recall success, back yourself and each other).

Players draw upon their physiological state or the 'feelings' they have about a situation to help form confidence. For example, a racing heart rate and sweaty palms could indicate fear and self-doubt, or being psyched up and ready for a particular task or performance. Accordingly, how one perceives these feelings will influence the confidence expectation one has (see also *Chapter Seven* on *Controlling Your Emotions*). Perceiving these feelings positively can facilitate cricket performance.

Positive emotions including happiness, exhilaration, and tranquillity are more likely to enhance confidence expectations than negative emotions such as sadness, despair, and depression. To illustrate, emotions such as fear and dejection experienced before an important game by a cricketer may be accompanied by symptoms of anxiety, which may be interpreted as indicating a lack of ability to perform a certain task, which in turn forges low confidence.

Finally, it has been suggested that imaginal states can also influence confidence. Imaginal states refer to the pictures or sequences of events we see in our mind. Indeed, players can generate confidence by imagining themselves or others performing successfully in an up and coming cricket competition. Thus, individuals who imagine themselves doing well in the lead up to an important game, innings, or bowling spell will have enhanced confidence in comparison to those who imagine failure or poor performance. One strategy which we introduce later to enhance self-confidence is that of imagery.

Alongside some of the theoretical sources of confidence (as outlined by Bandura), for some international and domestic players alike, an important source of confidence comes from their preparation. Indeed, many elite cricketers draw a significant amount of confidence from the quality and specificity of their training (e.g., when playing in the sub-continent - spending time on turning wickets, against quality spinners), their current level of fitness, and their injury status. In addition, just doing the things that you usually do (routine) can give you confidence.

In cricketing terms your attitude will also impact upon the way you and teams do things. This is true for both games and practice. Players with the 'right' attitude are generally seen to apply themselves effectively to whatever is asked of them and give 100% in every scenario. These positive people are willing to work hard and always believe that they can do it. Strangely in life, if you *believe* that you can do something then you are far more likely to succeed than if you feel that you can't make it, or won't be successful. So, it makes sense that positive people are more likely to be successful, because deep down they think they will be. They will always look to find a solution to a problem (even in the most difficult situations).

In summary, there are many sources of confidence that we, as individuals and teams, can draw upon. The real trick to becoming successful players and teams is to have a range of sources of confidence to draw upon, so if they are not in good form, or the stats are not great, or things doesn't feel good - they are still getting their confidence from somewhere. In the following section we explore the effects of confidence on cricket performance.

The Effects of Confidence on Cricket Performance

Whilst we have already highlighted some benefits of confidence in relation to cricket performance, in this section we outline more explicitly how confidence levels influence performance.

First, confidence influences cricket performance by helping determine levels of motivation, which will be reflected in the challenges individuals and teams take. Players with higher confidence will choose to undertake physical challenges and activities, and set goals that are more challenging than those players with lower self-confidence beliefs. For example, consider Tillakaratne Dilshan and his development of the 'Dilscoop' or 'Dilshan' shot. Indeed, it takes a very high level of confidence to consider developing such a shot in practice, let alone actually use it in competition on a regular basis, and under the utmost pressure.

Second, confidence has also been suggested to influence the amount of effort players and teams will expend along with their levels of perseverance. Generally, individuals and teams with high confidence will work harder, in both training and games, than those with low confidence. Think back to our example earlier about Manchester United scoring late goals. One possible explanation for this trend is the maintained level of effort they expend because of their high team confidence.

In terms of perseverance, players with confidence will always keep trying to develop and perfect their skills rather than give up or become complacent. Consider Kevin Pietersen and his well-publicized problems against left-arm spin bowlers. Rather than ignoring the fact that perhaps his technique had some glitches, he spent many hours working with his coaches and sport psychologist in practice scenarios batting against left-arm spinners to develop a technique that allowed him to be more successful. This is an example of a confidence behaviour.

Third, confidence beliefs also influence certain thought patterns (e.g., goal intentions, worries, responses to success and failure) and emotions (e.g., pride, shame, happiness, sadness) that also influence motivation. Individuals and teams with high confidence are believed to move on and learn from their mistakes and failures rather than dwell on them. Essentially, highly confident people are reflective practitioners, meaning they reflect effectively following training and performance to enable themselves to develop and maintain confident beliefs. To illustrate, by identifying areas where they have done well, and areas where they could improve, they are ultimately building their autobiography of sporting success and in turn learning their recipe for success (see also *Chapter Seven* on *Controlling Your Emotions*). The following quote from Michael Jordan, the famous North American Basketball (NBA) star, indicates how highly confident performers deal with failure:

"I have missed more than 9,000 shots in my career. I have lost almost 300 games. On 26 occasions, I have been entrusted to take the game-

winning shot...and missed. I have failed over and over again in my life, and that is why...I succeed!"

In summary, individuals with high self-confidence work harder, persist in tasks longer, and achieve at a higher level over and above people who doubt their capabilities. As we shall see in the next section there are numerous strategies that you can learn, and use, to develop your confidence in a way that helps you to reap the benefits we have identified.

Enhancing Self- and Team Confidence

Dealing with confidence-related issues is one of the most common areas of work we do with cricketers and cricket teams. For the most part this is because of the importance that role confidence has in relation to performance, but also the fact that confidence fluctuates. Indeed the old sporting cliché of *"Form is temporary, but class is permanent"* was almost written to reflect the fluctuating nature of sport confidence. Help is at hand, however!

Because of the important and significant relationship between confidence and sport performance, sport psychologists have extensively researched strategies to develop both individual and team confidence. Encouragingly, there is evidence suggesting confidence can be enhanced by using techniques which influence the various sources of confidence information as outlined in Bandura's model earlier in the chapter. Theoretically, by targeting various sources of self-confidence information with specific techniques - it should be possible to elevate and maintain confidence beliefs. In the following section we outline how techniques including imagery, modelling, self-talk, feedback, and hypnosis can be used to enhance confidence.

Imagery

Research demonstrates that individuals with high confidence maintain images of successful performances. Indeed, there is also increasing evidence that imagery (or visualization) can have a positive impact on self-confidence, although the type of imagery that players use is important.

One of the most effective types of imagery is for players to recall success. *Best performance imagery* requires players to think of a game, innings, or spell of bowling where optimal performance was attained. They then write a narrative for this situation in as much detail as possible (recalling thoughts, feelings, weather, and pitch conditions etc.) into an imagery script. This imagery script is then practiced until a player can imagine the scenario either with their eyes open or closed.

Best performance imagery can be used whenever a player feels it appropriate to boost their confidence. Typically, players may engage in imagery prior to batting, following the call from the captain to get loose prior to a bowling spell, or in the days leading up to an important game.

Theoretically, the real strength of this type of imagery is that it taps into the most important source of confidence information as outlined previously in Bandura's model - *past experiences*. Please see the best performance imagery task at the end of the chapter (Resource 6.1); it will help you to develop your own imagery script.

The key aspect to any mental skill is to practice. Indeed, we advise practicing the imagery script daily, for 15 minutes, for at least two weeks before it is integrated into training and performance routines. Another effective type of imagery is for cricketers to imagine themselves effectively coping with, and mastering, challenging situations (e.g., a bowler would learn to imagine to be able to cope successfully with bowling the final over, or delivery, in the final of the Indian Premier League tournament). Again, similar to a *best performance imagery* script, a narrative could be developed that outlines either a time when a player had coped well in the past, or one that takes a more prospective view where the script is based around future performance(s) or situations.

Modelling

Observing competent players successfully perform skills and tasks conveys important confidence information to other players about the sequence of actions one should use to succeed. Furthermore, observing a player (of a similar skill level) will generate self-confidence (providing the cricketer being observed is successful) along with motivating the observer to perform the task to the best of their ability.

In short, by observing similar skilled players succeed, observers' self-confidence and team confidence will be raised which may motivate individuals to try the task, as they believe that if others can succeed (e.g., peers, team mates) so can they.

Arguably, the most effective method of modelling is to self-model. This may involve a player recording their own performance (either in practice or competition), or completing a series of cricket tasks or skills that they perform successfully (e.g., playing the hook shot or taking a catch in the slips). The player subsequently views the tape as part of their preparation for games to boost their confidence by providing key past experience and modelling experiences information. This technique is also useful for coaches to provide confidence enhancing feedback to their players. The following quote highlights how such self-modelling is used by some cricketers:

"Before the Trent Bridge Test, he had had 10 days without an innings in the middle, so he spent an hour watching his big score at Lord's 'to get the blood flowing, and rekindle good memories'. In the bus back from the ground to hotel at the close of play, the whole squad watched a video of personal highlights during the day's play. Smith thinks this works well, even with those who have had a bad day; they try always to find something good for everyone." Mike Brearley writing about Graeme Smith (South Africa Cricket Captain)

In some recent work with an elite leg-spin bowler self-modelling was achieved in the following way. First, six training sessions were video recorded, then these recordings were edited into a final version that included the bowler demonstrating positive behaviours whilst bowling (i.e., effort and persistence), along with successful bowling performance (e.g., line and length, spin variations, and consistency). Initially, the player viewed the tape twice a day for 10 days prior to each game, as well as 2 hours before the start of each game in order to increase their confidence through the provision of important past experiences information.

Self-Talk

While talking to yourself is often jokingly considered to be the first sign of madness, many cricketers make use of positive self-talk to maintain or enhance their confidence levels. When used properly, positive self-talk can direct attention to task relevant cues (see also *Chapter Three* on *Staying Focused*), raise confidence and prevent the possible debilitating consequences of self-doubt (often due to negative self-talk).

In essence, self-talk taps into the verbal instruction source of confidence information as outlined in Bandura's model. A simple, yet effective way to develop positive self-talk (which can be used prior to, during, and after cricket practice and performance) is to go through a self-talk task.

Essentially, a player writes down any negative self-talk that they may experience and then comes up with positive responses that boost their confidence. See Table 6.1 for an example of how this may be achieved. These statements can then be placed on cue cards that players keep in their wallet or cricket bag. Prior to, and during, performance they may read or recall the positive self-statements to enhance confidence along with aiding their focus on relevant cues and thoughts.

The *type* of verbal instruction that coaches and other teammates use can also influence confidence. In essence, coaches may wish to consider the type of verbal instruction they provide prior to, during, and after training sessions and games to develop or maintain players and their team's confidence. For example, in a team-talk, prior to the start of an important game, it is key for coaches (through their verbal instructions) to encourage effort and persistence, remind players of success and their qualities, and remove any negative connotations (e.g., discourage negative self-talk such as *"Don't mess up"*; see also *Chapter Four* on *Performing Under Pressure*).

Table 6.1, Developing positive self-talk.

Negative Self-Talk	*Confidence Building Positive Self-Talk*
"I can't bowl on flat pitches."	*"I am good bowler and have bowled well on flat pitches in the past."*
"The umpires are against us - we will never win!"	*"There is nothing we can do about the umpires - if we focus on our game and play well then the umpires won't matter."*
"I am struggling to score runs at the moment and don't know which way to turn."	*"I have been successful in the past and have scored runs. I have to keep working hard in everything I do and the runs will come in time."*

Hypnosis

Recently we have used hypnosis as a way of enhancing players' self-confidence. Hypnosis is a process that uses the influence of suggestion(s) to bring about changes in thoughts, perceptions, feelings, memory, and behaviour(s).

Suggestion is an important facet of hypnosis and refers to the issuing of verbal statements (i.e., words and metaphors of how a person would like to think, feel or behave). For example, a leg-spin bowler may wish to feel calm, relaxed, confident and focused when standing at the start of their run-up, spinning the ball from hand to hand.

Hypnosis can be effective in enhancing self-confidence because it will impact upon all of the sources of self-confidence as outlined by Bandura.

- With regards to past experiences, the use of hypnosis can help a cricketer to recall previous mastery experiences, and imagine future ones
- Hypnosis can be used to provide information on modelling experiences. Moreover, a player can be presented with suggestions that relate to the successful performance or confident behaviours of a teammate.
- Hypnosis can generate effective verbal instruction (i.e., positive self-talk), so that suggestions can be given to provide player encouragement and support (which builds self-confidence about a particular cricket-related task).
- Hypnosis can impact upon physiological and emotional states (e.g., reduce anxiety and increase relaxation) as well as improve the imaginal experience (i.e., being able to imagine oneself performing effectively in games). This could be achieved via the use of suggestions to control and alter perceptions, emotions, and behaviour.

In addition to the direct use of psychological skills, as outlined previously, there are a number of alternative strategies that we have found during our applied work in cricket to impact positively on an individual's and team's confidence.

Control the Controllables

The concept of *Controlling the Controllables* in cricket is perhaps best summed up by the following quote from Matthew Hayden:

"Any cricket player - any human being - needs to learn to cope with the things they can't control: the weather, the touring, the opposition, sometimes even your teammates and your own form."

One reason why individuals and teams often lose confidence is that they become anxious and distracted by factors that they cannot directly control. In other words, they focus too much on things they cannot influence including the weather, pitch conditions, or umpiring decisions (to some extent!).

Psychologists generally suggest that you should focus on those things that you *can control* when competing (e.g., levels of effort and concentration). There is nothing to be gained from worrying about the things that you can't influence (e.g., opponent's preparation, quality/difficulty of the pitch, weather conditions).

By focusing on what they have to do to perform well (i.e., factors within their control), players are more likely to feel confident.

However, cricket is competitive and of course winning is important. Because skilled cricketers are good and display high levels of confidence, most of the time they perform well and when they perform well there's a greater chance that they will win. Nevertheless, it is impossible to say that every time they perform well *they will win* because there is always the chance that, on any given day, their opponents may perform that little bit better.

Essentially, the first step to winning is to play well. Confident players and teams are more likely to play well, and one reason for this is that they typically focus on factors within their control.

'Be a good coach to yourself'

Typically, in our work within cricket we find that players (and coaches) have a tendency to speak to themselves in a manner which is unhelpful and very different to how they would talk to others in similar situations. For example, following an unsuccessful performance some players will berate or beat themselves up, consistently reminding themselves of their failings and what a poor player they are.

In essence, it is beneficial for players and coaches to be good coaches to themselves. To this end, they should think about how they would communicate to a fellow player and coach in cricketing situations (e.g., provide encouragement, build confidence, provide reassurance) and thus adopt this approach when talking to themselves.

We find that players who can adopt this approach are often more consistently confident, but are more philosophical about cricket and the fluctuating nature of success and failure (see also *Chapter Four* on *Performing Under Pressure* and strategies for smart thinking).

Chapter 6

Body Language

During a cricket game, players and spectators alike will make judgements about how confident a player is on the basis of their body language (e.g., how they walk out to bat, deal with a mistake, and cope with pressure). A player who walks out to bat slowly, with their head held low, and tension across their brow immediately gives information to their opponents that this player is anxious and uncomfortable. In comparison, a player who jogs out from the pavilion shadowing shots, head held high, and chest pushed out displays confidence and calmness.

In essence, in our work we encourage players to pick a role model of someone who they think has good, positive body language and simply copy them. We want them to act confidently even if, inside, they may not feel it. The real benefit of this approach is that it will influence the perception that opponents have about a player to hopefully give them a slight advantage.

Over time, by acting like a confident performer, one will also start to think like a confident player. Good body language does not just relate to how one approaches the wicket. Think about how good players deal with distraction? Typically, they stop a bowler in mid-approach by the raising of a hand and a pulling away from the crease. Good players deal with mistakes by not replaying failure in their body language. For example, a batsman who plays and misses, will not replay the poor shot when shadowing the shot, but will rehearse what they should have done - thus giving off confident information to themselves but also creating a perception of confidence and control to their opponents.

Confident players also have good body language under pressure that may range from a wry smile to a cheeky wink. Our advice to players when entering pressure situations is to smile. First, no one ever expects people to smile under pressure, let alone look like they are actually enjoying it. Second, smiling releases feel-good hormones into our bloodstream making us feel calm and upbeat.

Of course, many of the examples illustrated above can also be applied to team behaviours and responses to success and failure. Accordingly, good teams always celebrate the fall of a wicket together, appeal for a decision together, and support each other when things do not go their way (see also *Chapter Ten* on *Building a Successful Cricket Team*). The importance of body language in cricket is perhaps eloquently illustrated by the following quote from Ian Bell:

"As I passed Shahid Afridi on the way out, he said I looked positive. I thought that's what you need to look like. That's what the people I talk to have been saying, 'Stop walking out like a schoolboy and walk out, chest out, like you mean business. With a presence.'" Ian Bell after making 115 in Faisalabad against Pakistan.

Food for Confidence Thoughts

What you put in is what you get out. This adage applies to many situations in our life but importantly it can be applied to the type of materials we expose ourselves to when developing our confidence. A well-known sport psychologist in America, called Alan Goldberg, contends that players should feed themselves material that is high in confidence (including books, movies, and audiotapes). Essentially, feeding on nonfiction materials about how successful people have performed against their odds and excelled can inspire players, but more importantly help to foster confidence. Therefore, we encourage players to go out and immerse themselves in popular culture including movies such as Moneyball, the Legend of Bagger Vance, the World's Fastest Indian, Senna, and When We Were Kings.

Summary

Confidence is one of the most important psychological factors in relation to cricket performance. As we have seen in this chapter, confidence is derived from many sources of internal (ourselves) and external (our environment) information. In addition, increased confidence is associated with many benefits, including increased effort, persistence, and performance. By engaging in and using some of the strategies presented we hope you will be better able to benefit from consistent confidence, which allows you to enjoy the challenge of performing in cricket.

Remember that high confidence leads to good performance and good performance on most occasions will lead to success. In the following chapter we explore how to control emotions in cricket.

Chapter 6

Key messages:

- Confidence is one of the most important psychological factors in relation to success in sport
- High confidence means players and teams expend more effort, are very persistent, set challenging goals, and typically perform better than those with low confidence
- Confidence is primarily influenced by past performances, modelling experiences, and verbal persuasion
- Confidence can be enhanced by a variety of techniques including imagery, self-talk, modelling, and hypnosis
- Confidence is also about controlling the controllables, being a good coach to yourself, and the presentation of good body language

Further reading:

Dweck, C. S. (2006). *Mindset: The new psychology of success.* New York: Random House Publishing Group

Goldberg, A. S. (1998). *Sports slump busting: 10 steps to mental toughness and peak performance.* Champaign, IL: Human Kinetics.

Advanced reading:

Bandura, A. (1997). *Self-efficacy: The exercise of control.* New York: Freeman.

Barker, J. B., & Jones, M. V. (2006). Using hypnosis, technique refinement and self-modeling to enhance self-efficacy: A case study in cricket. *The Sport Psychologist, 20,* 94-110.

Woodman, T., & Hardy, L. (2003). The relative impact of cognitive anxiety and self-confidence upon sport performance: A meta-analysis. *Journal of Sports Sciences, 21,* 443-457.

Self-Confidence Resources

Resource 6.1, Best Performance Imagery Script.

Being in the right *mindset* prior to, and during cricket, is an extremely important aspect of your preparation. It increases the likelihood of performing well and producing a successful performance. Indeed, a variety of techniques and strategies exist to help you prepare and develop the right mindset.

One strategy which can be effective in this regard is recalling and picturing occasions when you have performed particularly well. This, in turn, can be controlled through the use of imagery or visualization. For example, recalling a memorable performance will increase your belief about an up and coming match and so further focuses and enhances your mindset.

Like any skill, imagery requires a period of training and practice before it can have a beneficial effect on your mindset and performance. Therefore, we encourage you to practice your imagery of your best performances for 15 minutes, every day, for a week before integrating it into your cricket preparation.

Developing a Best Performance Imagery Script

You are now going to develop a best performance imagery script to use before cricket. First, write down a situation when you performed well. Now we want you to begin to recall as much detail as you can from your chosen example. It is important that you recall as much positive information about your performance as you can.

Now, recall the thoughts and feelings you were having at the time and note these down. In essence, the more detail you can provide - the more vivid and realistic the image will be, and the greater the effect on your mindset and performance. Once you have this information you can begin to compile your script that you will then begin to practice.

Chapter 6

Example of a best performance imagery script

This was an important final ball where 4 runs were needed to win and you were batting.

> Recall the confidence and belief you have as you stand at the crease staring at the bowler as he runs…….recall the clarity in which you see the ball leave the bowlers hand and make its way down the wicket….feel yourself quickly move into position as you quickly, decisively and confidently judge the line and length….feel the solid contact your bat makes with the ball on the half volley….hear the sound of the ball coming out of the middle….see the ball disappear quickly and accurately through the covers and over the boundary rope….feel yourself punch the air with joy after overcoming this difficult situation……recall the pleasure and feelings of knowing that you've just been successful……recall your coach and teammates running over to you and congratulating you on your success…….recall the feeling and thoughts of knowing that you are good….recall the feelings of excitement, pleasure and confidence as you walk into the pavilion and analyze what you have just achieved.

As you can see, visualization scripts typically include precise detail, contain pauses for thought and are always positive. Using the example as an aid, begin to develop a best performance imagery script for yourself. Once you have completed the script you may wish to record this onto your phone or PC so that you can listen back to it during your practice.

You should now go away and practice this routine for 15 minutes, daily, for two weeks.

7

Controlling Your Emotions

"Failure can lead you into a deep dark abyss of gloom and depression." Steve Waugh

"It's a mix of high skill levels and being clear mentally, strong minded. With the noise and pressure it's about how you control your emotions." Ashley Giles

Cricket is an emotional experience. It has the ability to make the hairs stand up on the back of your neck, to make you exude confidence, and to make you downright grumpy; all within a day's play. Indeed, when we involve ourselves in the sport of cricket we sign up to experience a vast spectrum of feelings from an abundance of joy and happiness gleaned from an important match victory, through to the terrorizing anxiety when preparing for a cup final, to disappointment and dejection following a defeat. Whether we want to experience these internal feelings or not, they happen. Thus, in order to optimize performance it is crucial to make the most effective use of our emotions, whether we perceive them as positive (e.g., happiness) or negative (e.g., frustration). This optimization skill refers to being in control of your emotions, and happily it is an element of our cricket we can develop, as Yuvraj Singh has found:

"... if someone says something, you want to reply, but you realise he is trying to get importance out of picking a fight with you. So then I think, I look and I move. Normally we react emotionally, so I try to keep my emotions in check. I can't do it every time. This is something I have changed about myself, because in the past I would always react. Then I figured that not saying anything can sometimes be more powerful than talking."

How we feel, and the intensity, or strength of these feelings, is unique. In other words, emotional responses differ from individual to individual in terms of what emotions are felt and to what extent they are experienced (i.e., a little to extremely intense).

Whilst individuals have various ways of controlling their emotions (to varying degrees of success!), different strategies may be required by different individuals and also for the same individual in contrasting situations. We hope the following chapter will help you in the quest of emotional control as it's not just about keeping negative feelings in check, but also strengthening and effectively utilizing positive feelings for your development.

What are Emotions?

Emotions are feelings we experience in response to an event or stimulus (which can be real or imagined), for example: happiness at hitting a boundary four, or frustration at a poor umpiring decision. In this way, emotions are contextual in that it is your appraisal of situations that gives rise to an emotional response. To illustrate, believing you can't cope (this is an appraisal) with the importance of a cup final will lead to debilitating anxiety.

Further, emotional reactions occur rapidly and unconsciously meaning that feelings can present themselves unexpectedly or, at least, before we have had the chance to consciously assess what has happened. Think about the road rage that individuals display when another driver pulls out unexpectedly and cuts them up!

Given that emotions occur naturally in everyday life, and in cricket, it becomes paramount to understand that it is the perception of our own emotional state that determines the impact of the experienced emotions on thoughts, behaviour, and ultimately performance. For instance, a cricketer may believe it's natural to be anxious before an important cup final and decide to focus on enjoyment and seeing the match as a challenge. In turn, the cricketer is likely to be confident and demonstrate effortful behaviour.

You have a choice and are able to control your responses to the emotion(s) felt by *managing* anxiety, anger, or excitement. Drawing on a well-known example, during the 2005 Ashes series Ricky Ponting angrily berated the England dressing room on his way back to the pavilion after being run-out by substitute fielder Gary Pratt. It was not Gary Pratt that caused the angry response, it was Ponting's possible lack of control when experiencing feelings of anger. Accordingly, a fundamental principle of controlling your emotions is to remember that the way we *think* about an event determines our emotional reaction. It is *not* the event itself (see Figure 7.1).

Figure 7.1, The ABC model demonstrating how emotional reactions unfold.

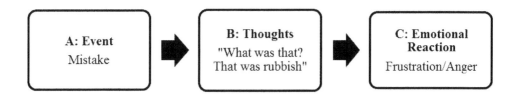

Emotions and Cricket Performance

As emotions are inextricably experienced by all of us, they can affect cricketing performance at any time. England captain Alastair Cook provides an interesting example of how professionals at the top of their game control their emotions and subsequently are more likely to perform optimally.

Cook's unrelenting levels of concentration, and ability to concentrate for long periods of the time, are widely recognized. Coupled with incredible focus is the England captain's equally impressive (albeit perhaps less well noted) consistency and the apparent stability of his emotions when he plays the game. To illustrate, after Cook led England to victory against India in December 2012, teammate Graham Onions commented how Cook does not typically elicit a lot of emotion but remains calm and composed following success and failure.

A consistent emotional state (e.g., remaining relaxed when he plays and misses), much like the emotional control of the great tennis player Roger Federer who appears calm and composed irrespective of the score, is likely to play a large part in Alastair Cook's consistent performances. It's important to enjoy the highs of cricket (e.g., scoring a century) and draw confidence from these successes but of parallel importance is the skill of letting a mistake (e.g., a dropped catch, bowling a wide) or adversity (e.g., the team not taking a wicket for a long period) go, without influencing how we feel. In this way, we aim to be emotionally consistent, which provides the right frame of mind to perform at our best.

Indeed, the ability to control yourself comes before the ability to control your performance. In turn, control brings more consistent performances and is the foundation of mental toughness as a cricketer.

Perhaps the most difficult cricketing situations in which to stay in control of our emotions are following adversity or failure, at a team or individual-level. Tough times ultimately make individuals and teams stronger. Indeed adversity, if worked through collectively and with the appropriate support, can develop resilience and bring teams together.

It can be useful to remind oneself how adversity breeds strength in potentially emotional situations (e.g., after a defeat). In the heat of the moment it may not feel like you will be able to learn from the experience or that the team will become closer; however, with time and commitment to personal development the despair will be seen in the overriding context of the highs and lows of cricket. To illustrate, the England test team had a difficult 2012, losing to Pakistan and at home to South Africa, but they were able to turn the momentum around and finish the year with a series win in India for the first time in twenty-seven years.

England's ability to manage their emotional states (e.g., to not become too anxious or frustrated) was important, but so too was using the emotional feelings conjured from the defeats earlier in the year in a positive manner. To achieve this swing in momentum it's likely that the England team were aware of their strengths and weaknesses, but continued to focus on, and play to, their strengths. Also, drawing on previous team (e.g., winning the Ashes) and individual (e.g., five wicket hauls in the past) successes, together with putting the defeats into perspective (e.g., no team wins every match) will have contributed to the upturn in performances and results.

Cricket will always be emotional and arguably we wouldn't want it any other way. For example, it's entirely normal to get angry from time to time, but if it's affecting your cricket performance, and/or situations away from cricket, then you may wish to think about your thought patterns and the events causing anger.

Here, we return to a key point stated at the start of the chapter: emotional reactions do not occur due to the event but thanks to what individuals tell themselves about the event.

In addition, we may wish to more effectively utilize, or channel, the emotions we are experiencing. Using emotions in a positive and constructive manner will enhance performance and indeed emotions may, on occasion, spearhead behaviour and performance. Take former Australian fast bowler Brett Lee for example; his clear desire, passion, and stern emotional energy were there for all to see (including the opposition). Being almost on the 'edge', as Lee was, and being so pumped up would enable him to unleash delivery after delivery at consistent high speed. Meanwhile, the batsman facing Lee would be influenced by Lee's behaviour in a way that was likely to increase the likelihood they would be dismissed.

Tread carefully with your own performance, though. Lee's aggression was on the edge but under control. If it was allowed to get out of hand (and the same is true for many pace bowlers) such strong emotion is likely to be detrimental to performance.

An awareness of yourself, and an understanding of whether your emotions are facilitating or hindering your performance, is crucial. Such self-awareness is necessary as emotions are inherent throughout cricket and developing skills to make the most of your natural emotional responses will increase your enjoyment of the sport, maintain your temperament, and aid performance.

The relationship between emotional responses and performance, however, is not clear-cut. Every cricketer is an individual and Brett Lee's emotional approach to pace bowling worked for him, but it's not the only way. In contrast, Monty Panesar personifies a more relaxed and calm approach. You may have noticed Monty Panesar glancing at a wrist watch before he bowls certain deliveries. Indeed, it is likely Panesar is checking his heart rate to ensure it's at the optimum rate to execute his next delivery as best he can. If he has become overly excited (e.g., appealing for a dismissal) or frustrated (e.g., being hit for consecutive boundaries) he will take a couple of deep breaths to reduce his heart rate and remain composed. If too high, heart rate will affect his co-ordination. If too low, heart rate will mean a reduction in his effort levels.

There is no one way to control emotions. But there is a *my way* – a way that works for you. Aim to understand yourself and delve into the techniques discussed at the conclusion of this chapter to become aware of your optimum emotional state, then utilize appropriate strategies to make the best use of emotional experiences.

Being aware of your strengths and weaknesses as a cricketer is important for personal development and is often emphasized by coaches. It is about knowing when you are experiencing emotions and how different emotions make you feel. In turn, effective self-awareness is understanding what situations or events in cricket typically give rise to an emotional response, whilst analysing whether these emotions help or hinder your cricket performance (that's the key question!). The idea of having an awareness of your emotions is referred to as emotional intelligence and is discussed in more detail in the strategies to develop emotional control, below.

Although frequently changing, emotional reactions can linger in cricketers' minds for long periods of time. To illustrate, positive responses (e.g., after a recent success) can be a blessing. We can take the positive feelings, together with the successful experiences into forthcoming matches. Negative responses (e.g., after a recent failure, getting injured or being dropped from the team), can linger and subsequently burden cricketers if strategies are not in place to learn from the performance and move on.

Typical negative feelings may include disappointment, frustration, anger, and the ability of these emotions to remain in the mind is enhanced when the emotional response in the moment (e.g., as the opposition hit the winning runs in a tight match), is strong. It is at this initial point that emotions are heightened and the intense reaction can result in the vivid recall of what happened after the event, and the disruptive maintenance of negative emotions in the mind.

In some instances the negative emotional energy has a productive motivational response as cricketers revisit the scenario in their mind, draw out and analyse the positive and negative aspects, and reinvest effort by continuing to train hard, approaching the next match in the same mindset (if not more motivated) as for the previous match.

Alternatively, some cricketers may dwell on specific mistakes or team failure and allow only the negativity to occupy their thoughts. Such a response, which is not uncommon, reduces confidence and hinders performance as cricketers vividly re-play (i.e., imagine) failure (and the associated emotions) in their mind.

Therefore the importance of aiming to appraise success and failure similarly is heightened in order to bring about positive behavioural consequences. Table 7.1 provides a summary of typical emotions experienced playing cricket, together with the potential consequences. We say potential consequences because you have a *choice* in terms of how you respond. Although we have grouped the emotions into stereotypical negative (the first five) and positive (the remaining seven) emotions, you can see that the consequences of each emotion do not have to correspond with the typical perceptions of that particular emotion. In other words, a negative emotion can aid performance (if we perceive it that way; refer back to the ABC model in Figure 7.1).

Chapter 7

Table 7.1, Typical emotions experienced in cricket and positive and negative consequences.

Emotion	When	Consequences
Anger	After being hit for 3 consecutive boundaries	**Negative** Red mist takes over the mind leading to poor decisions. Positive Use emotional energy to reinvest effort and amend plan (if necessary).
Despair	After a narrow defeat	**Negative** Wallow in what might have been (e.g., "What if?"). Positive Reflect on what went well and move on.
Frustration	Playing and missing	**Negative** Beat yourself up leading to uncalculated and risky strokes. Positive Use emotional energy as a cue to restart your routine.
Disappointment	Cricket match has been cancelled due to the weather	**Negative** Continuing to think about what you missed out on (e.g., playing cricket, or scoring big runs). Positive Think about whether the event was controllable or not. If it wasn't, there's nothing you could have done; if it was controllable then what more could you have done?

Guilt	When you nick a ball but don't walk and are not given out	**Negative** Continue to think about the fact you didn't walk.
		Positive Take it as a cue to restart your routine for the next delivery.
Content	Having a sandwich at the tea break after a good innings	Positive You are composed and prepared for the rest of the game.
		Negative Are complacent and do not plan for the rest of the game.
Pride	Coming top of the season averages	Positive Motivation and confidence to continue to work hard.
		Negative Become complacent and arrogant and don't practice as hard.
Happiness	At taking a wicket	Positive Enjoy the moment, reinvest effort and focus on next delivery.
		Negative Get carried away and forget the plan to the new batsman.
Joy	At making your international debut	Positive Enjoy the moment and use as a springboard for improvement.
		Negative Become complacent because you "have achieved" and met the target.

Excitement	When you are looking forward to playing a cricket match	Positive Seeing the event as a challenge, aiming to enjoy executing the prepared plan. Negative Over excitement can lead to high levels of arousal; important cues are missed.
Hope	When chasing down a total in one day cricket	Positive Provides a motivation to work towards, and a focus. Negative Not fully committed: "We might do this... or we might not".
Passion	When playing against your local rivals	Positive Up for it and focused on the controllable aspects of performance, which spreads through the rest of the team. Negative Overly so, with an outcome focus (i.e., the result) resulting in feelings of pressure and increased likelihood that important information is not attended to.

The build-up to a cricket game can be a time when emotions are running free. When elite cricketers and Olympians reflect on their successes they tend to recall how nervous and emotional they were before competition, but once the game or competition began they became immersed in the task and executed their well-trained skills with no disruptive signs of anxiety.

If professional cricketers and gold medal winning sport stars are nervous before they perform, then maybe nerves are a good thing? A cricketer's emotional response comes down to their perception of the feelings they are experiencing during their preparation. To illustrate, some players perceive their anxiety symptoms (e.g., butterflies in the stomach) as helpful for performance, whilst others view such symptoms as being unhelpful and hence they have a negative perception of their anxiety.

Physically, anxiety is effective as the associated increase in heart rate can elevate cardiac output allowing more blood containing glucose and oxygen to be delivered to the working muscles and the brain. Take a moment to think about your best ever performance, it's likely you felt anxious beforehand and then perhaps felt great once you had bowled, or faced, your first delivery.

A crucial message is that we should expect to feel a little on edge. If there are no butterflies in the stomach at all then it's likely that the player is too complacent and they will not perform to their potential. The following quote from Jonathan Trott explains how he approached his test match debut:

"You also have to think, 'I might not play here again, so I might as well enjoy it'. With my debut at The Oval [in August 2009 against Australia] - I got out in quite bizarre fashion in the first innings, hitting it straight to short leg and being run out. A lot of players would have been happy with 40, but I was really upset because it was the most fun I'd ever had playing cricket - 35,000 people cheering every run!"

There is great variation in cricketers' methods of mentally approaching games. In the quote above, Jonathan Trott describes how he focuses on enjoyment when preparing to bat. In another instance, before the final day of the test series between England and India, knowing England needed a draw to win the test series, it was mentioned in the media how Trott enjoys pressure. The next day Trott hit 143, England drew the match and won the series. It is likely that if Trott was to think too much about the task that lay ahead of him (e.g., the millions of people watching on television, the importance of the last day's play), he may have felt anxious (or pressurized) in a bad way for performance.

Many individuals allow anxiety to take over. Negative aspects of anxiety (i.e., when we perceive anxiety to be bad) lead to self-doubt and, physically, are associated with feeling lethargic, tense, and heavy (not good for performance). One practical way to overcome this is to follow Stuart Broad's lead of doing high knees before each spell of bowling to let go of any tension and increase blood flow and heart rate. Or as a batsman, jumping on the spot and walking with purpose to the middle can be a great way to energize the body.

Returning to Trott's pre-match approach, by telling himself to enjoy the challenge and trust his preparation, Trott was able to turn the anxiety into a positive aspect of his mental preparation by perceiving the nerves as his body readying itself to execute (and enjoy!). There is great variation in cricketers' abilities to deal with situations in which they feel pressure (e.g., preparing to perform before an important competition), please see the *Performing under Pressure Chapter* for more information.

Strategies to Develop Emotional Control

Emotions are inherent throughout cricket at all levels and developing skills to manage and/or make the most of these natural responses will increase your enjoyment of the sport, confidence in yourself, and ultimately benefit performance.

"I look up to him [MS Dhoni] as he always keeps his emotions in check, no matter what the situation. He's an amazingly balanced human being." Virat Kohli

Reflection

In this quote, Kohli describes MS Dhoni as a balanced individual. When we talk of controlling emotions 'being balanced' is perhaps our ultimate aim. One simple yet effective way to be balanced and develop emotional control can be to complete a reflective diary after each game.

Reflective diaries are useful as they increase the likelihood of cricketers evaluating individual and team performances in an adaptive way, negating a primary focus on the things that went wrong. Typically, we remember the mistakes made, together with the emotional response (e.g., frustration), and that outweighs the positive aspects of performance. Reflecting on three specific positives and one area for improvement from your performance in each game helps individuals draw confidence from the successes (e.g., "*I bowled a consistently accurate line outside off-stump today*") and enables them to move on emotionally from the experiences by setting a controllable target to develop an area they want to improve (e.g., "*I became frustrated easily when I didn't take an early wicket*"). For more information please see the *Reflective diary extract* at the end of the chapter (Resource 7.1).

Also, over a period of time, an autobiographical collection of your cricket reflections will be created that will serve two functions. First, your successes will build confidence (see the *Playing Confidently Chapter*) and promote positive emotions; while second, there is likely to be a helpful and logical realization that things won't always be positive in cricket. Setbacks (e.g., poor form) and barriers (e.g., teammates leaving the club) will be detailed in your dairy, but your reflections will show that you've worked through the tough times and come out the other side.

When we reflect on events in which we responded intensely (e.g., anger at being dismissed), we tend to look back, lessons learned, and wonder why we reacted with such severity. Across all levels of cricket, the ups and downs level themselves out. Expect, and be prepared for both. Reflection can help you enjoy the highs and stop you getting too down when it's low.

Self-Awareness

Reflecting on your own emotional experiences requires an awareness of what emotions are and the subsequent behavioural consequences (see Table 7.1). As highlighted previously, the ability to understand your own emotions and the emotions of others is referred to as emotional intelligence. Understanding yourself, together with the situations that typically make you overly emotional is the first step to managing emotional responses and optimizing performance. Further, identifying others' emotions can be useful; for example, being aware when an opponent is worried or concerned, or if a member of your own team is anxious about a cup final, so that you can act upon this to maximize performance outcomes. It's likely the teammate would benefit from a few words of encouragement and support. Developing emotional intelligence means that we can use our (and others') emotions constructively to benefit thought processes and cricket performance. For tasks to develop emotional intelligence please see the *Emotional intelligence tasks* at the end of the chapter (Resource 7.1).

Cue Words

Emotions produce natural energy that, when channelled, can be adaptive for performance. Cue words can be a useful way to utilize emotional energy in a positive manner.

As we have established, the emotional response occurs automatically, and so it is how we react when a specific feeling arises that we can control. At this stage it is paramount to occupy the brain (i.e., give it something to think about) otherwise the emotion (e.g., anger) will transcend throughout the brain to influence the decisions we make and the behaviour (including performance) we display.

Cue words or statements provide a useful task to occupy the brain and fill the void. For example, a player may get angry with umpires when they, in their mind, don't give a batsman out when they should have. If, in this situation, the brain is left to its own devices it's likely the player will continue to berate the umpire (either verbally or in his own head—"*They should have given that out*"), which only serves to intensify the feelings of anger to a point where the player reacts inappropriately (e.g., shouts at the umpire). At the same time performance decisions are rash, uncalculated, and more likely to lead to poorer performance. One reason for this is because the player is thinking about something that is outside of their control (i.e., the umpire's decision), and subsequently, the player is not in control of their emotions.

As stated previously, the anger response following the 'poor decision' is natural, but it at this point that a cue word or statement can allow cricketers to think and act more rationally, and with logic, to reinvest the emotional energy as motivation. Using cue words will distract the brain from the anger by giving the brain a controllable focus but what the focus is, specifically, depends on the individual (see also the *Staying Focused Chapter*). One example may be a statement such as;

"*That's gone now, focus on the next delivery*", which is more likely to manage the feelings of anger (rather than intensify them) and lead to an effortful and controlled next delivery. Table 7.2 provides additional examples of negative statements and corresponding positive statements that could be used in their place.

Imagery

Being in control of the words and statements you use in your mind (also referred to as self-talk) is fundamental to controlling emotions. In a similar way, so too are the pictures and images cricketers see in their mind when performing (referred to as imagery, see *Chapter Six* on *Playing Confidently*). As we mentioned in the previous chapter, imagery affords individuals the ability to take themselves away from the situation causing an emotional reaction. To illustrate, players can imagine being on a sandy beach and such images can function to relax and compose individuals when they feel emotions are getting out of control.

Table 7.2, Examples of negative statements and the corresponding positive statements.

Negative statements	*Changed positive statements*
"The umpire should have given that out."	*"That's gone now, focus on the next delivery."*
"What a rubbish delivery that was."	*"That's gone now; I know I'm good enough."*
"I never score runs here."	*"Enjoy the challenge."*
"This umpire never gives us anything."	*Focus on what you can control: "I'm going to give my all and enjoy today's game."*
"I'm stressed out."	*"It's okay to feel like this. This is my body readying itself for performance; focus on your routine."*

The majority of people 'imagine' every day. For example, on the way to work you may be picturing what you will be working on that day, and thus imagery is a technique that can be integrated into performance.

It is important, when using imagery, to ensure you feel sufficiently confident to control the image and to spend time practicing using all of your senses (i.e., sight, sound, touch, smell, and even taste) to make the pictures as vivid as possible. Indeed, you are in control of what you imagine. In other words you can be the director of your own pictures.

Although imagery can be used in training and competition, it can also be effective when not physically playing cricket. In terms of emotional control, you could spend five minutes a day visualizing yourself in cricketing situations where you typically lose control of your emotions; see yourself responding in a positive way. Imagining more constructive reactions will result in the brain seeing the new reaction as the 'normal' routine or habit, while you are likely to feel more confident in your ability to control your emotions. Ultimately you will increase the likelihood that you actually respond in a positive way in the heat of the moment.

Music

The use of music to aid sport performance is becoming more and more popular and is particularly relevant for emotional control. It is now commonplace to see sportspeople (e.g., Olympian Michael Phelps) walk out into performance arenas with headphones on, allowing them to listen to music in the dressing room right up to when they are about to perform.

Using music to help you to prepare for performance is a great (and enjoyable) way of promoting positive feelings and getting yourself into the zone.

Specifically, music can help us to concentrate on the task we are about to execute, it can motivate us (e.g., on the way to training), it can relax us (e.g., if we are feeling tense before we bat), and uniquely, particular songs can have meaning that produces vivid memories of the past. In this way, if we listen to songs that we associate with happy memories then this will make us feel happy and composed. It can give individuals a sense of comfort and reassurance even in uncharted territory (e.g., when on tour).

Indeed, the type of music you select is important. If you tend to get overly nervous before matches, listening to slow tempo, rhythmic songs will help you relax, while, if you want to energize yourself, something that has a fast tempo will help to get you fired up. It is well worth spending a little time developing your own playlist (see *My music playlist* at the end of this chapter; Resource 7.1).

Chapter 7

Focused Breathing

The stop/start nature of cricket permits time for players to release unwanted emotions or kerb the severity of such feelings. The lulls between deliveries, drink breaks, and changes of innings, allow you time to use techniques to control your emotions and heart rate.

Focused breathing can be useful to control physical responses in addition to our emotions. Concentrating on and slowing down your breathing can help you to reduce unhelpful emotions (e.g., dejection) and become composed prior to, during, and following your cricket.

Focused breathing can be therapeutic and relaxing as, with practice, it becomes rhythmical. Deep breaths slow your thought patterns down and help clear the mind to aid decision making. As with any skill, breathing routines require practice before they can have a beneficial effect on your emotions and cricket performance.

Initially, it would be advantageous to find a comfortable place where you are unlikely to be interrupted. All breaths 'in' should be through the nose, with exhalation through the mouth. A constructive routine may include inhaling for a count of four, followed by exhaling for a count of four with a focus on the controlled rhythm of your breathing for as long as you feel necessary. For more information please see the *Deep breathing exercise* at the end of the chapter (Resource 7.1).

As you feel more confident that the breathing routine is having a positive effect (after a week or so) and you feel more composed more quickly, you may be able to shorten the routine and maintain the desired effect. In turn, you can aim to integrate the shortened technique into training (e.g., after a dropped catch) and competition (e.g., after being hit for a boundary) to help control your emotions. In our work with four elite cricketers, focused breathing was used as a way of controlling anxiety when batting. Over time the cricketers were able to reduce their heart-rate (anxiety) after only a couple of breaths, in-between deliveries.

To finish, a caveat. It takes time and practice to develop emotional control skills just like technical skills. Further, it is likely that the emotional response you wish to change is ingrained as you have reacted in that manner for years. It can be like breaking a habit. Therefore, be patient, and persevere to produce a new ingrained response to more effectively manage your emotions. And if all else fails, laugh:

"I think it's very important to laugh, especially when you are angry and aggressive, to just take the tension away, make the moment go away."
Yuvraj Singh

Summary

Emotions are feelings we experience (in and out of cricket) in response to an event, which determine our thoughts and behaviour. Emotional responses are automatic and rapid but are typically categorized as having a positive (e.g., happiness) or negative (e.g., anger) influence on cricket performance. As we have seen in this chapter, it is the *perception* of our emotional state that gives rise to our (positive or negative) response. Accordingly, by practicing and implementing the strategies covered at the end of this chapter you will be better able to control, and make the most effective use of, your emotions for performance.

Key messages:

- Cricket is an emotional experience and therefore players will experience both positive and negative emotions. Positive emotions (e.g., happiness) can bring about helpful performance gains, while negative emotions (e.g., anger) have a debilitating effect.
- Emotions occur as a consequence of an event or stimuli in our environments
- To develop emotional control in cricket, players should consider the use of reflection, cue words, imagery, and music
- The ability to control emotions effectively allows players to perform more effectively in cricket

Chapter 7

Further Reading:

Thatcher, J., Jones, M., & Lavallee, D. (2012). *Coping and emotion in sport* (2nd ed.). Abingdon: Routledge.

Advanced reading:

Jones, M. V. (2003). Controlling emotions in sport. *The Sport Psychologist, 17,* 471-486.

Totterdell, P., & Niven, K. (2012). *Should I strap a battery to my head? (And other questions about emotion).* Printed by Createspace.

Controlling Emotions Resources

Resource 7.1, Strategies to develop emotional control

Reflective Diary Extract

> I hit a couple of well-timed cover drive boundaries when batting.

> I bowled a consistent line at the top of off-stump during my first spell.

> I executed my pre-delivery routine before most deliveries and this helped me to stay composed and focused.

> I became frustrated when I didn't take an early wicket when bowling. To improve this I will reflect on what I am telling myself in the situation and introduce a more positive and constructive cue word or statement.

Chapter 7

Emotional Intelligence

Emotional intelligence tasks

There are a couple of tasks that could be useful to complete at your next training session.

First, tune into the emotions you are experiencing throughout your practice. Make a note of these, following training, and importantly detail what event/situation was associated with the emotional response (e.g., excitement at being told to pad up). Also, think about what you were telling yourself about the event and appraise how constructive this was.

Second, think about your teammates' behaviours and reactions to events and consider what emotions they are experiencing. This will help you tune into how your opponents are feeling.

My Music Playlist

Track & Artist	Feelings	Memory	When
e.g., Artist X – Track X	Ready, motivated, focused.	Used before we won the cup final.	Before I go out to field.

Chapter 7

Focused Breathing

Deep Breathing Exercise

---

1. Find a quiet and relaxing place where you are comfortable and will not be disturbed.

2. Breathe in deeply through your nose and out through your mouth as follows:

  Inhale through nose: COUNT IN, TWO, THREE, FOUR

  Exhale through mouth: COUNT OUT, TWO, THREE, FOUR

  Focus on a part of body that feels relaxed (e.g., fingertips)

3. Repeat this routine for as long as necessary (e.g., 10 minutes).

Initial practice of the breathing exercise should be on a daily basis, for around 10 minutes.

8

Leadership and Captaincy

"A captain must make every decision before he knows what its effect will be, and he must carry the full responsibility, not whether his decision will be right or wrong, but whether it brings success." Don Bradman

"The captain has to pull together ten different individuals with contrasting personalities and personality traits and get them all going in the same direction by treating them equally but differently." Steve Waugh

"I think with captaincy you just have to do it your own way. You can't copy someone. You can learn from different captains as you go along but in the end you have to follow your instincts and do the job the way your character allows you to do it." Alastair Cook

In all effective cricket teams there needs to be a number of leaders. Depending on the level of the team this could include coaches, captains, vice-captains and 'informal' leaders both on the pitch and in the dressing room. The bowlers also need to have well-developed leadership skills to be able to set their fields and to liaise with the captain. All teams need to have a sense of direction, strategy, and tactics that are determined and driven by the leaders in the team.

The captain plays an important leadership role that is involved in selection, making decisions on the order of play (so winning the toss and whether to bat first, the batting order), determining the strategy of the team (the tactics that are employed) and making calls regarding when to change field placings. He or she also makes bowling changes and generally seeks to influence and control the game. In order to achieve all of these role requirements, the captain needs to be an effective leader, able to man-manage all the different characters and personalities that make up their team. The captain also needs to be able to inspire the team to follow them and in many cases look to lead from the front. There is an old maxim that says "*If you preach excellence but walk mediocrity, you are nothing but a liar*".

Also, to be a good leader you also need to understand what it is like to be a follower There is nothing worse than having to cope with energy sapping players as a captain. So an important aspect of leadership is man management. Finally, as a leader you need to be able to resolve conflict when it arises in your team. Disharmony in your team is a sure fire way to poor performance. This chapter will explore the different approaches to understanding leadership, and the role of the captain in more detail.

What is Leadership?

Due to the very nature of leadership, and its application across many different areas and domains, there are many differing definitions. For example, leadership can be described as "The process of influencing individuals and groups toward set goals". Alternatively, it can also be described as "Knowing what should be done, and influencing others to cooperate in doing it". This second definition in particular suggests an importance in the *understanding* and *experience* of the leader as well as demonstrating important leadership behaviours.

This process of defining leadership is further complicated by the fact that a good manager can be a good leader, but a good leader does not necessarily become a good manager. Looking at the differences between good leadership and good management there is a slightly different focus for each. The partnership between Andy Flower and Andrew Strauss for the England test team could be considered a perfect combination of a good leader and a good manager. Management is to see, as a bottom line focus, how certain things can be best accomplished; in essence doing the right things. Leadership looks at the top line, what are the things we want to accomplish; essentially seeing what the future might look like. In order to become a good leader, you need the ability to be able to plan, organise, and control. Leadership is a concept that allows for both horizontal and vertical applications.

Within cricket teams there are two clear types of leadership role: formal and informal. Informal roles are those that emerge within the team as a result of interactions between teammates and the demands of the game.

The team is influenced by the actions of players who are the most dominant, assertive or competent. These informal leaders can help to set the tone for the team. Formal leadership roles are those that are prescribed or awarded. Examples of which include coaches, captains, and sometimes vice-captains.

In general terms formal leaders have two main responsibilities. First, to ensure that the *demands* of the team/club are satisfied and that the team is effective in terms of the goals and objectives set. The second responsibility of every leader is to ensure that the *needs* and *aspirations* of the team are fulfilled. Indeed Ex-England captain Mike Brearley highlighted that the captain can be responsible for how long people practice in the nets, who needs what practice, alternative options for rainy days, travel arrangements for away fixtures, and many others things as well. Indeed, the captain often ends up putting the rest of the team's needs ahead of their own. If not managed effectively, this can take its toll on the captain's own performance.

A number of theories have been developed that have tried to explain leadership and how leaders develop. The first theories focused on something called the 'great man' approach. This approach has got the longest history and focuses on the character of great leaders. The view here is that if you identify what it is that great leaders 'have' you can start to develop a template for the 'type' of person who needs to be the leader (the captain). This approach suggests that leaders are born and do not develop. However, whilst appealing on the face of it, evidence suggests that there is not a specific character type that is best suited to leadership. If you looked at successful cricket captains you would probably find that they are very different people, but all good captains in their own right. As a result a second theory of leadership was developed.

This second approach looks to see what 'type' of leader a particular situation required, suggesting that certain situations called for specific types of leaders. So, match the leader to the situation and they will be most effective. However, this approach has also been challenged.

A more appropriate third approach is to consider the personal qualities required for leadership. What do different captains do that make them successful? Also, what are the personal qualities that the situation requires? This is important as the same team can require different types of leadership at different stages in its development. A team in transition will require very strong leadership and direction. But as the team becomes more established, and the team members are more settled, this type of approach can be damaging to the team. In this instance a more democratic and inclusive approach is required.

There is also the consideration of what works best for the leader, and what works best for the team? In an ideal situation the leader's approach and the approach the team would prefer are the same. But in some situations that is not the case. So the question emerges, which is more important? That the team is led in the way they would like (even if the captain is not very effective in that approach), or the team is led in the captain's preferred way (even though the team may be less happy)? There is no definite answer to this question, but it does need to be considered by the leader.

The Effects of Leadership on Cricket

There are four main effects which general leadership may have on your cricket. First there is the degree to which you, as an individual, show personal leadership both on and off the pitch. Second, there is the degree to which you are well led by your captain in the team. Third, if you are a bowler there is the degree to which you take the lead in arranging your field settings and making tactical decisions. Finally, there is the leadership and direction offered by the coach.

The Role of the Cricket Captain

Captaincy, like coaching, varies significantly depending on the team and the level the team plays at. Cricket differs greatly from many other sports when you look at the role of the captain. In soccer the captain is a formal leader on the pitch and a role model off it, but the way the team plays and the major decisions taken during a game are determined by the head coach. In cricket, on the other hand, the team is very much the captain's to lead. The captain makes all the decisions on the pitch and is part of the formal leadership of the team off the pitch. An effective captain is invaluable to the team and its performance outcomes. They will seek to lead by example, to motivate and to inspire the team to successful performances.

In general terms, captains are selected based upon their experience, their level of performance and often the position that they occupy in the team (often batsmen).

There are, in essence, three main responsibilities that captains have for the team.

1. To act as a liaison between the coaching staff and the team
2. To act as a leader during all team activities (particularly on the pitch)
3. To represent the team at events, meetings, and press conferences

Alongside this there are a number of specific roles that captains perform. These include:

- Ensuring a constant flow of information between the coach and team
- Leading by example
- Inspiring and motivating
- Helping the coach in the planning stages for the team
- Conducting oneself in a professional manner before, during and after the game with respect to teammates, opponents and officials

Important skills for captains to master include:

- Being effective communicators
- Remaining positive (regarding performance, potential and outcomes)
- Controlling one's emotions
- Remaining respectful to fellow players and coaches (setting the standards that all others are expected to meet)

Mike Brearley in his very good book "The art of captaincy" highlighted the sacrifices that the captain often makes within the team. While the role often rewards them with influence and standing in relation to the task - there is often a social cost. Brearley specifically highlighted the difficulty of being 'one of the boys' and engaging in normal banter and gossip like the rest of the players in the team.

Chapter 8

As mentioned above, in cricket - a captain's role is enhanced compared with other sports. Captains not only fulfil a leadership role, but also fulfil a management role making decisions on strategy and tactics, selection and planning, as well as determining who bats where in the order and who bowls when. The size of the role is further compounded by the sporadic use of vice-captains in cricket. This absence of a co-leader in many cricket teams makes it difficult for the captain to delegate responsibilities. In many clubs and teams the vice-captain is appointed as someone who can 'stand-in' for the captain if they are not available. The most effective teams, though, select vice-captains who complement the captain - helping them to lead the team. They are not necessarily selected because they are going to be the stand-in captain, but rather to offer a trusted opinion to the captain, to offer a different point of view, and to offer a different route through which communication can take place.

Also, it is important for captains to recognise that they don't need to do it all themselves. Very good captains will maximise the usefulness of the players that are in their team. So, the captain's strengths might be in being very organised and by planning well, but not being the best at coming up with a new plan when everything else is not working. If there is someone else in the team who is good at being innovative in the field then the captain can use them for ideas. Often captains feel they need to do it all themselves, whereas they just need to remind the team of thoughts which relate to playing well. Think of it this way: the captain is steering the ship but does not have to be rowing the boat at the same time.

Now, you might ask the question 'How do I know what the rest of the team can contribute?' Well, this comes down to the way that you lead. If you are always 'leading from the front' and making all the decisions you might never know what some teammates might be able to bring to the team. However, if you ask colleagues for their thoughts and ask questions such as 'What would you do?' or 'What do you think?' you can start to get a feel for how the rest of the team thinks and what they might be able to contribute. This approach also has the added benefit of empowering the rest of the team to think in more detail about the game and to feel a greater sense of ownership into the courses of action the team ultimately takes.

Becoming a better Leader and Captain

A number of factors have been highlighted that appear to distinguish the most effective leaders. These include:

- Being effective in doing what is required of them
- Ensuring a high degree of satisfaction within the team
- Continually helping, and supporting fellow players to develop their physical and mental abilities to ultimately improve team performance

Leaders can also seek to increase their influence or power within the team by paying attention to their appearance (looking professional), demonstrating self-confidence and expertise, appropriately allocating rewards and sanctions, and being a role model for the team to try to emulate. Regarding appearance the leaders should 'model' the accepted dress code (and this relates to how clean and professional they appear). Furthermore, the team are more likely to follow someone who has expertise and prior experience relating to the task in hand; a successful track record as a player is a great start to gaining the respect of the team.

The leader needs to have confidence in their own ability and be confident in the tactical choices that they make. Portraying an air of confidence will make others feel confident. But by the same token, if you do not appear confident this will be transmitted to the team and they, in return, will feel less confident.

The leader is also responsible for the allocation of rewards and punishments. The degree to which this can be done consistently and effectively has a direct impact upon the power that the leader has with the group. If you are not consistent or appear to be weak then you will not be well respected, and ultimately effective, as a leader. Being an example for others to try to emulate (a role model) is also important. Team members are far more likely to follow someone who leads from the front or who has the relevant experience - than someone who does not.

In addition to the above, effective leaders have also been shown to engage in the following behaviours:

Chapter 8

Continue to develop interpersonal (man management) skills

Interacting with other people is crucial to the role of the captain in cricket. In particular verbal and non-verbal communication skills are central to this.

Work towards building a cohesive team

How 'together the team is' has been highlighted as a key determinant of performance and team effectiveness. As such the leader should be looking to enhance this togetherness where possible.

Listen well

This is linked to effective interpersonal skills. Listening is crucial to building good relationships, and relationships are central to leader effectiveness. As a result, learning to understand people in greater detail is crucial.

Make strong decisions and be willing to be accountable for those decisions

In order to be most effective, leaders need to have a plan. They need both the determination to do it their way and prove willing to accept responsibility for the ultimate success or failure of the plan.

Are active and direct problem solvers

Active problem solving requires a pragmatic approach focusing on the direct issues that need resolving. Dealing with issues when they arise reduces stress in the long-term as issues do not drag on unresolved.

Create standards for performance

Effective goal setting and quantifying successful performance is also important. Developing minimum standards of behaviour and performance is a key component of an effective team. Crucially linked to this is the need for the team to buy into these performance standards and to not necessarily see them as imposed.

Recognize and reward generously

Reward and praise are important tools for the leader to use. The consistency and equality of these is also important. Consistent approaches giving clear messages and guidelines to the team are important. As a result the consistent meaning of rewards and praise is enhanced.

Convey enthusiasm

A key role of the leader is to motivate and empower the team. As a result the leader needs to adopt a positive outlook on situations as this, and the leader's demeanour, will be transmitted to the rest of the team. Similarly, the leader's enthusiasm and positivity will be transmitted to the team. If the leader is defeatist and downbeat this will also be conveyed to the team.

Teach relevant skills

Often the leader also needs to act as a coach to 'up skill' members of the team so that they can fulfil their role and cope with the demands placed upon them. Sharing knowledge and skills is important to empower individuals within the team, but also creates a closer bond between individuals.

Use punishment as a last resort, but make punishments clear at the start

The development of rules and boundaries is important. Crucially these should be developed and communicated at the start. This way the team is aware of the punishment associated with relevant behaviours. This prior development of punishment also removes the emotion from the decision making process should team member(s) have broken team rules for behaviour.

The captain in a team also plays a very important role in mentoring younger players, and as a result is particularly important in providing information, support and guidance. He or she is an on the pitch leader as well as an off the field representative for the team, occupies a potential role model position, and needs to adhere to a standard of behaviour both on and off the pitch that is reflective of the values of the team and/or the club.

The captain also needs to lead by example in *game situations* in relation to the style of play, environmental factors, and umpiring. They will also act as a source of inspiration and motivation to the rest of the team. As a result, developing each of these areas is important to be effective.

It is important to remember that a successful team is built upon a series of successful individual performances. Due to this, an effective captain needs to value the performance and input of all team members during the game/performance. The ability to influence all members of the team in slightly different ways either before, or during, a game is a key characteristic of truly effective captains. Also, as with other forms of leadership, the ability to empower others is crucial to ultimate success. Good captains will look to develop the knowledge, understanding, and confidence of their bowlers, for example, to empower them to take the lead in determining their field settings and tactical decisions when bowling.

Man-Management

Another important aspect of effective leadership and effective captaincy is your ability to work with individuals. This 'man management' is crucial. We all know that there are different types of people, and as a result different sorts of players. Some players are very extraverted (loud and talkative) while other players might be introverted (think more, and like their own time and space). Some players make decisions based on logic and reason while others prefer to go with their gut instinct. There are those who want to understand the bigger picture with other players who are happy focusing on the here and now. A truly effective captain and leader needs to be able to understand and communicate with all of these different types of people. This is important because what motivates one person will not necessarily motivate another. The key is to be able to get the most out of each individual player.

Central to this idea of man management is the ability to build relationships and to get to know people. You will not really know the best way to talk to a player, or how to motivate them, if you do not first take the time to get to know them. This, in turn, requires you to ask questions to find out about them and to actually listen to the answers they give. Now this might seem like a strange thing to say but it is important. There is significant evidence that what actually happens in most conversations is that two people talk *at* each other and have almost their own separate conversations. This is because, for many people, they use the break in their speech to think about *what* they are going to say *next*. Unfortunately this also happens when the other person is talking, and as a result you don't hear everything that each person is saying. So, the first step in effective man management is getting to know the other person through listening and actively making an effort to get to know them.

Once you listen and learn, you will start to develop an understanding of what makes a person 'tick', and in doing so will know what their strengths, preferences and weaknesses are. You can then start using this information to get the best out of each individual and out of the team as a whole. This is most important when the team is not doing very well.

When a team is winning it is far easier for players to stay motivated and to be committed to the team. This is far more difficult when the team is not doing so well. The captain needs to be able to 'take the team with them' and prove able to resolve any issues that arise on an individual basis with the relevant players. This can only really be done through knowing the individual. Otherwise there is the potential that you have the opposite effect and either demotivate, alienate or patronise the other player, which will be detrimental to the team going forward.

Communication

We communicate all the time, but are not necessarily aware of the messages that we are sending. Understanding the nature of communication in the team can help to develop strategies to enhance the team thanks to improved communication. This is important as a lack of good communication can result in a lack of cooperation, reduced coordination, and increased confusion amongst the team.

Of particular interest to cricket teams are *interpersonal* and *group communication*. Interpersonal communication is simply communication that takes place between two or more people. Group communication refers to communication that takes place between a number of individuals who are members of the same group or team.

Communication can also generally be further divided based on whether it is verbal or non-verbal, and whether it is intentional or unintentional. Verbal communication, as you would probably expect, is quite simply communication through the use of spoken sounds and words. Central to this are the words that you use to *express yourself.*

Non-verbal communication is a generic umbrella term that includes a number of specific components. These include:

- Facial expressions
- Eye contact
- Body language and posture
- Physical appearance
- Proximity (how close you are)
- Gesturing
- Touch

Non-verbal communication is very important in cricket. The captain (in the field) uses gestures to direct the fielders. Also, umpires use signals and gestures to give a batsman out, signal a four or a six, wides, no-balls and free hits.

Good communicators need to be aware of both the verbal and non-verbal ways they communicate to be really effective leaders. If your mouth is saying one thing, but your body is saying another - the strength of the message you are trying to communicate is lost. So to be most effective as a communicator you need to ensure that verbal and non-verbal communications are *saying the same thing.*

Intentional communication (as the name suggests) relates to messages you deliberately mean to send. An example of this is when the captain uses their finger, to point to where they want a fielder to move to, on the pitch. Unintentional communication occurs when individuals inadvertently send messages that they did not mean to. Body language is a good example of this. In a game when performance is going against you in the field, heads and shoulders can drop; this in turn sends a clear message to the batting team, who will seek to capitalise. It will also make the batsmen feel more confident which will make your job harder.

All aspects of communication can be improved. If you are not great at sending the right messages non-verbally - work on practicing the relevant behaviours to send the right messages. You can also become more aware of the non-verbal messages you send through video analysis where you watch back how you present yourself.

A good example of the use of non-verbal communication is through 'active listening'. This is where you demonstrate you are interested and engaged in what the other person is saying. You can achieve this by sitting forward, sitting still, looking them in the eye, nodding, and focusing on the person you are listening to. If you laugh, or look away, or yawn, or fidget then you are just encouraging the other person to stop talking. As a result you might never know what they thought or had to say.

Finally, many captains, coaches, and leaders in general, often search for the 'golden' team talk. The sort of thing that you see in the movies. This is where the leader (who has usually been through some degree of hardship) is able to stand up and give a speech that both motivates and inspires the team to win (and inevitably the team then goes on to win). As a result many captains get side-tracked by the wrong question. You should not be asking 'How do I give an inspirational and motivational speech?' Instead, you should be asking 'How do I motivate and inspire the team?' These two things are definitely not the same thing.

Some people are naturally great speakers, so for them, talking to the whole group might just work. However, for most people, they should look to inspire and motivate each individual player separately. This can, in part, be achieved by leading by example (be an inspiration). This can also be achieved by understanding what makes each player in the team tick and being able to motivate and inspire them based upon their personal philosophy and values. This represents more work for the captain (you need to get to know all of the team), but can ensure that you are able to both motivate and inspire the team through effective man management.

Chapter 8

Resolving Conflict

A key aspect of any leadership role is the ability to resolve conflict. In cricket teams there is always a degree of 'banter' in the dressing room. But sometimes this banter can go too far, or players can fall out either on, or off, of the pitch. To ensure that the team keeps on being as effective as possible, a key job for the captain is to help defuse and resolve these potential conflicts.

But it is also important to remember that conflict can also be helpful rather than just a hindrance. Whilst conflict *might* harm performance and the togetherness of the team, it can also help the team to question current approaches and practices driven by a desire to move forward. So, in a sense, conflict can be both constructive and destructive.

Teams should look to encourage constructive conflict while reducing destructive conflict. Constructive conflict has been shown to be beneficial to teams as it can enhance team decision-making quality and acceptance, increase performance and lead to a greater degree of creativity and innovation. The main sources of conflict in a team relate to differences regarding the task at hand, and personal/relationship conflicts.

Task conflicts can include different viewpoints, ideas, and opinions. Relationship conflicts usually arise because of an incompatibility between teammates and can include tension, animosity and annoyance.

In conflict situations, one of the roles of the captain is to defuse, manage and resolve the situation. Five specific approaches to conflict resolution have been identified in the psychology literature:

1. Collaboration
2. Competition
3. Accommodation
4. Avoidance
5. Compromise

The approach adopted depends upon the people involved.

Collaboration In this approach you should state your views, listen to the other party's views, and then come to a negotiated solution. In this approach the solution should incorporate the views of both parties and be acceptable to both parties.

Competition In this approach the two parties have differing views regarding the situation and the relevant solutions that are either available, or desirable. It is up to one party to convince the other party to accept their point of view, and ultimately their solution (either/or).

Accommodation In this approach, whilst both parties have differing views regarding the issue and potential solutions, you deem there to be strategic reasons why accommodating the alternative view or solution is advantageous.

Avoidance In this approach the issue that forms the basis of the conflict is largely ignored, hoping that with time, the issue will resolve itself.

Compromise In this approach both parties have different viewpoints, but are willing to make concessions in order to resolve the issue.

Summary

The leadership that a team receives is fundamental to the team's success or failure. This is true for, coaches, captains and informal leaders. Effective leaders influence, inspire, and motivate both individuals and the team. Mike Brearley has suggested that fundamental to the role of captain is the desire to understand what makes people tick.

Whilst understanding the characteristics of the individual and the situation are important the *interaction* between the two appears to be critical to success. The more the captain is aware of the situational demands the more likely they are to be successful in a variety of environments. As a result, the self-awareness of the leader and in particular their style, strengths, and weaknesses appears to be important.

Chapter 8

Understanding the tactical aspects of the game is important, but even more so is the ability to communicate, organise, make decisions, man-manage, and resolve conflicts. So, captaincy should not just be about the best player, but about the best leader. Sometimes, these are not the same thing.

Key messages:

- Leadership is an important aspect of cricket
- There is no one approach that works best, play to your strengths as an individual
- Get to know each individual and become an effective man-manager
- You don't need to have all the answers, make sure you use all the skills of your team
- Always look to lead by example
- Pay particular attention to your communication skills (including listening)

Further reading:

Brearley, M. (2001). *The art of captaincy*. London: Channel 4.

Cotterill, S. T. (2012). *Team psychology in sports: Theory and practice*. Abingdon: Routledge.

Covey, S. R. (2004). *The 7 habits of highly effective people*. London: Simon & Schusler Ltd.

Advanced reading:

Judge, T. A., Bono, J. E., Ilies, R., & Gerhardt, M. W. (2002). Personality and leadership: A qualitative and quantitative review. *Journal of Applied Psychology, 87*(4), 765-780.

9

Preparing to Perform: Playing to Your Strengths

"Success is a process. During that journey sometimes there are stones thrown at you, and you convert them into milestones." Sachin Tendulkar

"When I was playing the game we never had the benefit of TV or video to analyse our techniques or look at faults, we depended on other cricketers to watch us and then tell us what they thought we were doing wrong." Geoffrey Boycott

"I should like to say that good batsmen are born, not made; but my long experience comes up before me, and tells me that it is not so." W.G. Grace

When you head out onto the pitch to play cricket there are two crucial things that you need to maximise to be successful. The first is that you need to have developed a good understanding of what your strengths are, as a player. Knowing this enables you to begin to develop effective tactics and strategies to achieve the most that you can. The second thing that you need, to be successful, is to have *practiced to perform*.

Now, you might think that 'I have done my training', but the real question is 'Was it the right kind of training'? You are most likely to be successful if you have practiced how you are going to play. The closer practice is to the real thing the better the transfer of skills and decision-making.

Cricketers often spend time trying to improve their weaknesses, but don't focus as much on developing their strengths. This, in turn, can leave a degree of ambiguity in their match plans. Understanding what your strengths are, and how you can most effectively play to them, is crucial. In this chapter we will explore the best ways to practice to play, and also explore why both understanding and playing to your strengths is not only desirable but *essential* for successful performance in cricket.

Preparing to Perform

We all know that to get better and become more consistent at something we need to practice it. There are many stories in the media, across a range of sports, which highlight the importance of practice.

In most cases this notion of 'practice' refers to practicing a skill to be able to execute it most effectively. In this context, practice refers to training, essentially training to get better. However, many individuals and teams go through the motions of practice without really knowing what it is that they are practicing for. Just being in the nets and hitting a few balls or bowling a few deliveries is not necessarily good for you.

It is said that practice makes perfect. That is not strictly true, *practice makes permanent*. The more you do something in a certain way the more it becomes reinforced and you develop a tendency to respond in that particular way to a stimulus (such as facing a bowler). The more you practice the more permanent or habitual this way of acting becomes. As a result, what you learn and practice in training forms the foundation for how you play in a match. Any good or bad habits you have in practice will more than likely be transferred to competition.

While this idea probably seems pretty straightforward and just common sense, many players and coaches do not consider this basic principle in their preparation. While many players will practice their skills in training they often do not practice in the same way that they play in a game. This could involve not preparing for each delivery in the same way, not looking to control emotions in the same way, and often not setting the same high standards, targets and goals. If this is the case and you do not 'practice as you play', you end up teaching yourself bad habits that will ultimately creep into your game, and these bad habits will surface under pressure when it counts.

Players are even less likely to practice or prepare for the specific scenario that they are going to encounter. One way to illustrate this is to think of how most people revise for an exam. There are generally two types of students when it comes to exams, those who revise and those who do not. Similar groups of players exist in cricket, so if we substitute the skills in cricket for the knowledge needed in an exam the story is the same. Students who don't revise significantly reduce the possibility of being able to answer the questions and to pass the exam. Cricketers who do not practice their skills significantly reduce the possibility of selecting the right shot and being able to execute the required skills. So, for both exams and cricket if you want to be successful it makes sense to be in the group that revises and practices.

However, both of these 'revision/practice' groups can also be split into two. In both examples the first people of these two groups (and the majority of the group as a whole) practice/revise in a comfortable environment. This is called a comfortable environment as it does not reflect the stress and pressure of the environment in which you are required to perform. Most exams take place in a cold hall, sat on a rickety chair at a small desk (why are the desk legs always uneven, making the desk wobble)? But the majority of students revising for exams do not factor this in and instead lie on the bed, or revise with friends, or listen to podcasts. All of these are useful, but don't reflect the demands of the task (sitting the exam).

In order to really prepare effectively these students should try sitting and working in a similar set-up to the exam hall, and practice answering questions (which is what they are going to have to do on the day).

This same viewpoint can be held with cricket practice. Most players practice by bowling or facing a few deliveries in the nets, but *don't really* practice for the environment in which they are going to have to perform. In both cases the small number of students/cricketers who do practice in this way (practice to perform) will be the most successful.

To be successful as a cricketer you need to ensure that your practice prepares you to play. Often the only way to achieve this is to create the scenario in your head and then play it out like in a game. Brett Lee, the Australian fast bowler, echoed this approach by saying *"Preparation became a lesson that I learnt as my career extended, I prepared very differently now to how I did ten years ago. Preparation is all about training your brain to be ready for the battle ahead."* This quote also highlights another important point, that often it is the quality of the practice rather than the quantity that is important. Evidence shows that what you do in practice is likely to be transferred to the game. As a result, allowing yourself to get into poor habits when training could expose you in the game.

What is Preparation?

Preparation is exactly that, preparing to perform. This is slightly different to skill development. Good coaches and good players will draw a distinct line between the two.

Skill development is a cognitive (thinking) process where the player is learning to execute a new skill or a new technique. This initial stage of learning is characterised by relatively high volumes of repetition where the player and the coach are trying to programme the player's brain to execute the skill in a certain way. Due to the fact that this is a process where the player is having to think about what they are doing, how it feels, and seeking to understand the differences between good and poor skill execution - other demands on the player should be minimised.

In comparison, preparation (or practice to play) should develop the player's ability to execute these skills under pressure. The crucial thing to remember here is that it is the *execution of the skills* bit that is important. If the skills have not been sufficiently learned, trying to perform these skills under pressure becomes very difficult. If you really want to be able to do it in a game you first need to be able to do it (the skill). So a bowler who wants to bowl yorkers in the final over of a T20 game first needs to have developed the skill and control to bowl yorkers. This is similar to the process that Pakistani fast bowler Wasim Akram went through. Akram when reflecting on his career highlighted that "*I had to learn to bowl the Yorker at will, not just now and again.*"

Once skills have been achieved the next step is to look to apply them in a game. In preparation to play, the aim is to test the player's skills (where possible) at the same *intensity* and *accuracy* levels as in a real game. The things (skills) that you learn in practice and preparation are the things that you are going to do when you get into a game situation. This is because, under pressure, we always revert back to our learned habits. That is one of the reasons why changing your technique can be difficult; you are always fighting against the technique that you have already learned.

To make sufficient changes to your technique you need to allow yourself time to learn the new skill (and to re-programme the brain) before the new technique can really be effective in a game. For the same reason if you always practice at 75%, you will probably play at 75%. If you allow yourself to get angry and frustrated when practicing, you are far more likely to get angry and frustrated when playing. The brain actually does not differentiate between the different environments. If you react in a certain way when you are getting the ball bowled at your head your brain will program you to react the same way when it happens in a game. If you don't practice your concentration (focusing) skills you will probably not be able to use them effectively in a game either.

Justin Langer and his batting mentor Neil 'Noddy' Holder used a Japanese concept called Kaizen to underpin Langer's practice. Kaizen can be translated as a strategy or attitude of 'continuous improvement', always looking to improve no matter what your level or ability. In his book 'See The Sun Rise' Langer reflected that this approach had enabled him to continue to get the most out of practice and to ensure he always maintained his quality.

The Effects of Preparation on Cricket

The crucial thing to remember about practice is that you are practicing your behaviours and your thought patterns for when you play. The best players will prepare with intensity, and also be very specific in what they are trying to achieve. Also, good players will look to make preparation *more challenging* than the real game environment. This approach to training pushes these players to have greater control, and greater accuracy. In this way you can make the execution of skills in the game feel easier than in preparation. Some players and coaches refer to this idea as 'practice hard, play easy'.

Returning back to the idea of forming habits, everything we do activates specific connections in the brain. The more we do the same thing the more we activate the same connections. The more we activate the same connections the more likely it becomes that (in the same situation in the future) you will activate those same connections to execute your cricket skills in a certain way.

So, if you practice dropping the ball (although it's not clear why you would) you get used to executing your movements to miss the ball. The next time the ball comes to you, even if you try and catch it, the chances are that you will drop it because your body is used to dropping the ball. Now, if you were really thinking about catching the ball you might be able to catch it, but once under pressure (in a game) your body will remember how to drop the ball, and as a result, will probably drop the ball.

There is significant evidence in neuroscience studies of the brain that the brain is always learning. It is better (from a learning perspective) to break a skill down or slow it down so the learner is successful (and learns success) rather than doing the whole thing at normal speed and learning/reinforcing failure. It works in the same way with the mental side of your game. After every ball in the nets, if you are always negative and focus on the things that were not so great - this is the behaviour that you learn and reinforce in your brain. In a match situation, you would start thinking negative thoughts for every delivery and then focus on things going wrong rather than the positives. This mindset is more likely to increase the number of things that actually do go wrong. In essence, a self-fulfilling prophecy.

It takes a lot of time and effort to become an expert in executing a skill. This expertise is characterised by near flawless execution time after time. It also takes a lot of time and effort to learn how to execute these skills in real situations and under pressure. This can't be achieved just by playing games, so you need to make sure that you use your preparation to reinforce the execution of the skills under the right conditions and challenges. Once you have learnt the skills, you need to learn how to apply them under pressure.

There is another important consideration here. This relates to what you are trying to practice at a specific moment in time. If you are practicing your skill execution and looking to enhance your technique - ideally you would look to do this whilst you are fresh. Tiredness reduces your ability to think and perform, and also reduces your ability to focus (see *Chapter Three* for further details).

Good quality practice for skill development and the enhancement of technique should not be overly long, with plenty of breaks and opportunities to recover to maintain a relatively high level of performance. This however changes if the focus of your practice relates more to practicing to perform. The assumption now is that your skills are as well learnt as they need to be, and the focus is on being able to execute these skills in more realistic environments and scenarios. One factor that is present as you play cricket is *increasing fatigue*. As such you might make the sessions longer, or (even better) do something else beforehand that increases fatigue levels, and then engage in the session. You could work to exhaustion on a treadmill, or by cycling, then go and try to execute your skills. This 'forcing' yourself to perform will help to build your 'resilience' for when you are in tough situations in a game.

Preparing Effectively

Preparing better is, at least in part, dependent on developing a good understanding of the challenges that exist in the real game performance environment. If you understand these challenges you can set up scenarios and challenges that, as accurately as possible, replicate the real thing.

Following on, the way that you construct practice is important. A batsman facing 30 balls from a bowling machine that are all reproducing bouncers is unrealistic. A batsman would never face that many bouncers in a row. We would expect the batsman to be playing them much better by the 20th delivery compared to the first delivery, but this is not realistic. Improvement would happen through familiarity with the task and trial and error. This point again comes back to whether the player is learning the skill or preparing to play. If you are learning the skill you need repetition to get better at the skill. When preparing to play you need to be able to play the one or two bouncers per over when they come along. So, preparing with real bowlers, who mix up the deliveries, is a more realistic scenario. Also, the bowling machine (while good for learning how to play the shots) takes the bowler out of the equation, so you do not learn how to 'know' when a short ball is coming. Without knowing what to look for - how do you know you will make the right decision? (See *Chapter Eleven* on *Effective Decision Making* for further information.)

Chapter 9

To make any scenario feel as real as possible it is the *responsibility of the individual player* to make the scenario as realistic as possible. Only the player can apply the relevant constraints and determine what acceptable performance is. Anything the coach sets up that is outside of the real game environment is never quite the same. It is the responsibility of the player (batsman, bowler, keeper, or fielder) to create the real scenario in their head and push the intensity levels required.

Anyone can hit a ball and think that it was all right, or bowl a delivery that is okay. The best players, in preparation mode, will have a specific scenario in their head and will have a clear idea of what the required outcome is. Then, after every ball, they will evaluate their performance against this target, with only the best being acceptable. In this way you learn to execute the skill, but also how to execute the skill in the right situation with the appropriate control.

Bowlers also need to practice the relevant scenarios. You can get very good at landing the ball in a certain spot, but part of the challenge is related to what the batsman does. You need to be able to react to the batsman's movements to win that competition and to have a plan B and a plan C that you can use when plan A is not being effective. In turn, coaches need to set up practice sessions that introduce realistic consequences. For example, in a batting change you can opt for the 'out is out' approach where the player has to sit out the practice or the nets for a period of time. This is a little more realistic than just batting on.

So what are the factors that characterise the aforementioned 'real' environment? A significant factor is the performance environment you are in. The closer you can get to the real game environment the better. So, practicing on a prepared grass pitch, in the middle, with batsmen, a keeper, bowlers, umpires, and the appropriate number of fielders in real game scenarios is about as realistic as possible.

Now, recognising that this is not possible a lot of the time, you need to think about how close you can get to this. So, for example, if you can't practice in the middle then in grass nets is the next best option. If this is not possible, then indoor pitches, or concrete pitches outdoors, are the next possibilities. Facing bowlers who bowl six consecutive balls, then change is the ideal set-up. The next step would be bowlers alternating every ball then if you don't have bowlers - using a bowling machine or throw downs. For the bowlers getting to bowl six balls in a row (and getting to 'construct' an over) is better than individual deliveries (when preparing them for the real game environment). That said, though, there is some very good scenario work you can do off a single ball (e.g., last ball of an innings, the batting team needs a four to win).

Another important factor in effective preparation is to ensure the presence of a keeper and an umpire. Research has shown that not having someone standing in the umpire position fundamentally changes the run-up of the bowler. So, without the umpire the bowler is learning something that is different from how they play the game. By not having a wicket keeper behind the stumps the batsman could be more likely to come down the pitch knowing that the consequences of missing the ball are not the same as if there was a keeper in place.

Another important aspect of scenario work is to try and create (as much as possible) intense *environmental conditions*. The England and Wales Cricket Board's (ECB) National Cricket Performance Centre (NCPC) based at Loughborough University has taken this idea to the next level by controlling the environmental temperature within the centre. As a result normal English conditions can be replicated, or alternatively the heat that might be experienced out in the sub-continent, West Indies, or Australia can be generated.

While this is not possible for the majority of cricketers across the world, the same principle applies. What environmental conditions are you going to face when you play? How can you best prepare for these?

Physical condition (as mentioned previously) is another aspect to scenario work. We have highlighted the importance of your general physical condition and how this relates to your ability to play, but we can also consider how these physical states are achieved.

Often when playing in the nets, batsmen just face ball after ball. This does not happen in a game. Thinking about a 'real' game, batsmen are out in the middle in pairs, and have to run and communicate (regarding when to run and how many). This should be reflected in effective scenario work.

Also, the way bowlers bowl can be less than optimal during practice. If a bowler in a game bowls six ball overs in spells of, say eight overs, then make them bowl similar workloads during scenario work. In turn, you need to consider the development of fitness-focused functions (such as strength and speed). Speed can be developed through running drills and strength through the use of free weights. But once developed they need to become functional. It is not really useful for a batsman if they are really quick in their trainers, shorts and a t-shirt, and slow in all their batting gear.

It is a similar story for strength. Being really strong is great, but if you can't exert that force through the bat it is not really useful. So, once you have developed the basics you then need to ensure that the benefits are communicated into the real application of your skills. Once a batsman is becoming quicker make them do drills in their batting gear. Testing them in their batting gear, using time trials over set distances, is a good cricket performance-related measure. With the strength aspect, try getting the batsmen to engage in range hitting (seeing how far over the boundary they can hit the ball). In this way the body gets used to recruiting the relevant muscles for the cricket-specific tasks they need to engage in.

An important aspect of setting scenarios in your head is the ability to 'imagine' the situation, and put yourself in it. Some players are very good at constructing an image (relating to the scenario) even with their eyes open. They can visualise the fielders, and possibly the crowd. This then helps when evaluating the performance, whether the delivery achieved its intended outcome, or whether the shot was successfully executed in the context.

One way to get around the very internal nature of imagining situations is to get players to verbalise (say out loud) the scenario, letting others (teammates and coaches) know the scenario, the position of the fielders, and what success would be in that situation. This achieves two main goals. First, to commit the player to the scenario (once we verbalise something it becomes more real). Second, it allows others to objectively evaluate the performance of the individual based on the scenario. This way the player is not able to allow themselves to 'get away' with it in practice.

To perform when it counts, in a game, you need to be able to construct your practice in the right way to give yourself the best chance.

Playing to your Strengths

We have all seen examples of players who are really good at knowing their own game. These players have a particular style of play or strength, and are very good at playing to these strengths. Indeed, playing to your strengths increases the likelihood of being successful. Brett Lee supported this when he made the point *"Your strengths are your most important weapon when taking the field."*

Linked to strengths is the idea of a player 'understanding' the way they go about their game. Understanding their mental state when they play well, for example, is really important. Good players take this a stage further by understanding the steps they need to take in order to get into this optimal mindset. It is the optimal mindset that allows them to play at their best and to play to their strengths.

Justin Langer was a strong advocate of the power of understanding your game, *"I have come to realise that one of the most important aspects of human development is the concept of knowing yourself. You are at your best when you understand exactly what makes you tick."*

Often, good players will control the game, and will make the game revolve around their strengths. This allows them to play the shots they are most successful with, and play to the areas where they have the greatest control and the greatest success rate (as a batsman). Bowlers will be able to bowl their best deliveries in their most dangerous areas. Captains can also be more effective if they understand the strengths of the players in their team. If you get the players in the right positions in the field to maximise their strengths - the team's fielding performance will improve.

Whilst it is important, when you are a young player, to have role models and heroes, it is also important to find your own way of playing. This will be influenced by both your physical and mental characteristics. Trying to play the game the way that another cricketer plays will never be as successful as figuring out what *your* way is.

In cricket, all too often, form turns out to be a temporary state. Sometimes you play well on a consistent basis, and at other times you do not play too well. All we know for certain is that no player can play well all of the time. But, for the players who know their strengths and know their game the gaps between playing really well (being in form) and being out of form will be reduced. This is because by understanding your game and the mental state that you need to play (and hopefully the strategies you use to get there) you can work yourself back into your ideal performance state.

If, however, you just 'let your cricket happen', then your form becomes a little hit and miss. When you are playing well that is great, but when your form deserts you - you don't know what to do in order to get back to playing well.

What is also important though is understanding what your strategy to get into your optimal mindset is. That way, when it is not just automatic that you will play well - you can take steps to significantly increase the potential for your form to return.

When you are going through a rough patch of form always remember what you have done historically rather than looking to find new solutions. Glenn McGrath, following a run of poor form, found this approach helped, "*I decided to go back to doing what got me picked in the first place, hitting good areas, getting a bit of bounce and seam movement, and going from there.*"

What are Strengths?

To understand what your strengths are, a good starting point would be to clarify what a strength actually is. In general terms 'a strength' is seen as an advantage that you possess. So your strengths as a player are advantages that you have in relation to other players.

More specifically, strengths are our natural ability to behave, think, or feel in a way that allows us to perform at our best. These strengths are partly innate (we are born with them) but are ultimately shaped by our environment.

It is also important to be aware that sometimes our strengths can also be our weaknesses. If, as a batsman, your strength is being able to hit the ball big back over the bowler's head - that is a good advantage to have. However, if you try and do this every ball then the fielding captain and bowler will put a couple of fielders out on the boundary and wait for you to mistime or mishit a shot (and as a result give your wicket away).

Alternatively, your big advantage as a bowler could be the significant number of variations that you bowl; but if you continually change the delivery every ball it becomes more difficult to effectively execute your skills. So, knowing your strengths is important, but also knowing when to play to them is also important.

The strengths for some players are more physically orientated (e.g., being a very powerful player), but strengths can also be technical (the timing of the shots a player makes). Strengths can also be mental (a bowler who is very good at making the right decisions under pressure), and strengths can also be emotional (you are very good at staying in control and not getting emotional). So, an important starting point for any cricketer is to understand the strengths they have, and how this makes them different to other players.

There is an important branch of psychology, called positive psychology, that has focused on understanding peoples' strengths. Findings from positive psychology research studies suggest that it makes more sense to focus on your strengths than your weaknesses. People (or players) can get even better at their strengths more easily than reducing (or trying to reduce) their weaknesses. So, whilst appreciating that we always try to reduce our weaknesses, maybe it is just as important to focus on what we are good at, and to get even better at that.

How does an understanding of strengths affect cricket?

Understanding your strengths, and the way that you play, fundamentally drives the way that you do things, from preparing to playing. What works for one cricketer will not necessarily work for another player. This means that it is difficult for a coach to adequately cater for every player all of the time. So, to be a very good player you need to take more personal responsibility and ensure that you get the things you need out of training, practice, and preparation.

To do this, you need to know what works for you and what steps you need to take to get there. For example, if you are a 'feel' player you will practice until it feels right. If you are a routine-based player then executing your routine will be the thing that makes you feel ready to perform.

Once you are clear on what your strengths are, you can use this information to form the basis of the tactical plans and strategies you develop for the game. If you play best when you are being an attacking and aggressive player then it makes sense to play in this way regardless of the situation. You would obviously moderate the specific application of this strength based on the situation, but the general template would stay the same.

Playing to your strengths will offer the greatest certainty that you will execute your skills effectively, make the right decisions, and crucially be able to execute those decisions.

Players who understand their strengths will, by definition, have a template against which they can execute their performance. This is because by playing to your strengths - you increase the likelihood that you will be successful. Why? Because you are less likely to make errors or fail to execute your skills correctly. This, in turn, increases the potential for a successful outcome.

Summary

Learning skills is only the first part to becoming a good cricketer. If you want to be a good cricketer you also need to practice how to execute these skills in the real game environment. You can (and will) learn when playing, but by preparing effectively you significantly increase the likelihood that you will be successful, and on a consistent basis.

The best are the best because they practice and prepare hard, but crucially they also practice smart. They look to get the greatest quality out of every delivery they face or every delivery they bowl. Linked to this is understanding one's strengths. Once you have a clear understanding of what your strengths are, you will be more confident, execute your skills more effectively, and make better decisions under pressure. You will also be able to develop effective strategies and tactics based upon your strengths. This in turn will increase your likelihood of success.

Key messages:

- You need to practice to perform, as well as practice to learn your skills. It is all about forming the right habits.
- Make the training environment as realistic as possible; that includes training under pressure
- Understand your strengths and look to play to these where possible.
- Good preparation increases confidence
- Playing to your strengths will improve your decision-making ability and increase the likelihood of success

Further reading:

Linley, A. (2008). Average to A+: Realising strengths in yourself and others. CAPP Press.

Advanced reading:

Gordon, S. (2012). Strengths-based approaches to developing mental toughness: Team and individual. *International Coaching Psychology Review,* 7(2), 210-222.

Roberts, L. M. et al., (2005). *How to play to your strengths*. Harvard Business Review: January.

10
Building a Successful Cricket Team

"Great leaders set the example. They walk the talk and they perform when the pressure is on. They also follow through with their vision and make things happen." Justin Langer

"A losing team tends to split into small factions and grumble about things, while winners stay a tight unit." Steve Waugh

As a sport, cricket is different and unique from most other team sports. Unlike many team sports, cricket involves aspects of behaving as a team, but also very individual performances when batting and bowling that are not dependent upon working effectively with teammates. As such, cricket, more than any other sport, has the dilemma of whether to focus on putting together a team with the most talented and effective individual players, or looking to build the most 'together' team that works most effectively as a 'unit'.

This particular dilemma exists across all levels of the game and has been around since the game began and the issue of 'selection' became prominent. This dilemma reflects the fact that a team of experts is not the same as an expert team.

As the game at the highest levels becomes even more competitive both clubs and teams are looking at how to build team performance. This is most apparent when teams are fielding - where they look to perform as a group and look to apply strategies and plans that involve all the players in the team. The body language of the team, the intensity, and the energy are all things that effective teams expect to see.

There are many examples in cricket where the most talented teams have lost to the 'underdogs'. This includes England losing to both the

Chapter 10

Netherlands in the 2009 ICC World T20 at Lord's, and to Ireland in the 2011 Cricket World Cup in Bangalore, India.

Often we see that groups of very talented individuals do not necessarily form the best teams. It is how well these individual players function as a whole that is most important.

All good coaches and managers will consider the 'fit' of new players to ensure optimal team functioning. Some coaches go one step further and will have a general template for the 'type' of players they want in their teams. This way you can look to build a team where the players are most likely to perform well together.

It is also important to recognise that different challenges exist for the coaches in both professional and amateur teams. To illustrate, an amateur coach is often required to forge the best team they can out of the players who are existing members of that club or team. Professional coaches have greater flexibility (they can change the playing staff), but these coaches then have to consider the impact that changing the personnel will have on their existing team.

An important starting point when looking to build an effective team is to clarify exactly what a team is. At a basic level, teams can be described as a collection of two or more individuals who have a common identity, are driven by common aims and goals, share a common fate (they win or lose together), have a structure and channels of communication, have similar views about the team, are linked to the group both socially and competitively, and consider themselves to be a team.

This description of what a team is clearly highlights a number of specific factors. Indeed, just by understanding this description of what a team is there is scope to enhance a team. Developing a common identity, developing clear goals, building good communication channels and developing an effective team structure are all good places to start. Steve Waugh, the very successful Australian cricket captain, highlighted similar factors that underpin successful teams:

"To me that 'X' factor that all winning teams and organisations exude and others try to emulate is best defined by the culture, character, camaraderie and karma that the group exhibits."

There are many important psychological factors that impact upon a cricket team. These psychological factors range from more general factors such as teamwork, to more specifically defined concepts such as momentum, motivation and communication. Further still, there are a number of factors that exist at an individual level, but which combine to become characteristics at a team level, such as emotion, mood and the performance psychology environment. Other psychological factors that can have an effect include the dynamics of the group, its leadership, and psychological recovery.

Many experts, both in cricket and in the wider sport community, talk about team building and its importance. Team building is the deliberate process of designing and supporting the development of an effective team. The aim of the team building process is to build a more functional team that can achieve greater levels of cricket performance more consistently, more of the time. By understanding the psychological factors that influence the operation and performance of the team a cricket coach, team manager, or sport psychologist can help to build the team to achieve higher levels of achievement and performance.

What is a Successful Cricket Team?

Success is a very subjective indicator of how well a team performs. If you just equate success to winning trophies then most cricket teams by definition are unsuccessful. In any given league or cup competition there can only be one winner, and if adopting the 'winning is success' approach then only one team can be successful in any given competition or tournament.

We think that the real measure of success relates to the aims and goals that the team sets for itself at the start of the season, or possibly during their pre-season planning. If the team meets, or exceeds those targets, then it is a successful team. So, a team that wants to maintain their status in a particular league (e.g., not getting relegated), or to reach the quarterfinals of a knockout cup competition, is seen as successful if they achieve these targets. This suggests that an important aspect of building a successful team is to have a clear process through which the goals, aims, or targets for the team are set (For more details on how to set clear and effective goals please read *Chapter Two* on motivation and commitment).

Success should also not necessarily be focused solely on outcomes such as winning or achieving a certain position in a league. Success can be the way that you play the game, and the degree to which you and the team as a whole stick to your principles for playing.

Successful teams have a good understanding of who they are, and what they stand for, this then becomes apparent in the way that the team conducts itself on and off the pitch. It could be that the most important thing is reflecting the 'spirit of the game' or looking to entertain the crowd by playing an exciting brand of cricket. All of these things, if achieved, might be viewed as success.

The Effects of Togetherness on the Team

There are a number of different ways in which the 'togetherness' of the team can impact upon performance. Indeed research suggests that there is a relationship between togetherness and performance. This togetherness is referred to as 'cohesion', and research has found that there is a reasonably strong relationship between cohesion and performance. Unfortunately, at present, it is not really understood in what direction this relationship exists. Do teams perform better because they are more cohesive, or are teams more cohesive because they are performing well? Intuitively you would expect this relationship between cohesion and performance to exist as it is easier to get on with other people in the team when you are winning and everything is going well. You are also far more likely to fall out and pick faults with your teammates if you are losing.

If you think of the different aspects of a game of cricket you can start to understand how the way the team performs as a unit can impact upon performance. First, think about the team in the field. Over recent years the fielding aspect of the game has changed significantly. Fielding has evolved from a relatively sedate exercise to becoming a very athletic component of the game. Fielding is now about saving runs as well as taking catches.

The top international teams now assess their fielding performances based on the number of catches dropped and runs conceded as well as catches taken and runs saved. The way a team fields determines the environment in which the batsmen are playing. This can be quite a relaxed and non-threatening environment, or can be quite hostile and threatening, which in turn can unsettle the batsman. Now you might be thinking that what we are talking about is sledging, and putting the batsman under pressure through chatting to them, but that is not the approach we are referring to. In particular we are interested in how the fielding team acts. Whether consciously, or subconsciously, we are always reading the body language of other people. It is how we know when someone is happy or sad without them telling us so. So when the batsman is at the crease they are continually getting messages from the opposition around them. This is generally referred to as non-verbal communication, and includes facial expressions, body language and posture, eye contact, physical appearance, gesturing, touch, distance from the other player, and the way you are facing.

Facial expressions are responsible for a huge amount of non-verbal communication that takes place in cricket. For instance, think about how much information can be conveyed with a smile or a frown. While non-verbal communication and behaviour can vary dramatically between sports, the facial expressions for happiness, sadness, anger, and fear are similar throughout the world. As a result, it is possible to read the emotional state of other players when playing (e.g., when they are getting angry or frustrated).

Gestures are deliberate movements and signals and are an important way to communicate in cricket. Gestures are particularly important when trying to communicate over longer distances such as to a player fielding out on the boundary (boundary riding). Common gestures include waving, pointing, and using fingers to indicate numerical amounts.

Posture and movement can also convey a great deal of information. Research in this area has focused in particular on the interpretation of defensive postures, such as arm-crossing, and leg-crossing. While these non-verbal behaviours can indicate feelings and attitudes, research suggests that body language is far subtler and less definitive that previously believed.

Chapter 10

The 'distance from the other player' refers to the degree of 'personal space' a player is enjoying. People often refer to their need for 'personal space' which is an important type of non-verbal communication. The amount of distance we need and the amount of space we see as belonging to us varies and is influenced by a number of factors including the culture we live in, the situation, the individual's personality, and how well you know the other person/people. For example, the amount of personal space needed when having a casual conversation with another person usually varies between 18 inches and four feet. On the other hand, the personal distance needed when speaking to a crowd of people is around 10 to 12 feet. A player wishing to make another cricketer feel uncomfortable can step into their personal space to achieve this effect. One example of this is when a fast bowler goes to speak to a batsman. In this instance, it is not the words that are important, but the invasion of the batsman's personal space and 'getting in their face' to make them feel uncomfortable.

Eye contact, specifically relating to looking, staring, and blinking can also be a very important non-verbal behaviour. Looking at another person's eyes can indicate a range of emotions, including hostility, solidarity, concern, interest, and intimidation. When talking to the team, the coach needs to continually make eye-contact with the whole team to make a connection and to convey the message. If the coach just looks at a small number of players this can be divisive.

'Touch' relates to communication through actual physical contact. The notion of 'putting your arm around someone' is an example of this approach. Also, teams congratulating each other or sharing positive emotions can be achieved through touch (such as high fives, touching fists).

Our choice of colour, clothing, hairstyle, and other factors affecting appearance are also considered a means of non-verbal communication. Research on colour psychology has demonstrated that different colours can invoke different moods, and even that the colour of a room can directly impact upon our mood. With this in mind, it might be worth painting the dressing room of the opposing team black if you wanted to put this into action. Appearance can also alter physical reactions, judgment, and interpretation of the situation. Knowing this, the messages that the appearance of you and your team communicates to others (e.g., supporters, opposition) is very important. Individuals who attempt to communicate their individuality and difference from the team will often achieve this by individualizing their appearance.

Another factor mentioned earlier in this chapter is the idea of giving energy to the team. Good teams talk about having 'energy' in the field, and actively look for ways that each player can give energy to the team. This can be achieved vocally and focused chatter in the field for good teams gives the team a positive lift. But this chatter has to be targeted. Teammates should be trying to be motivational and encouraging, and provide positive feedback to their teammates when they do something positive. Teammates should be supportive if a teammate makes a mistake. This fulfils two main functions. First, it helps to keep motivation and effort levels high in the fielding team (and as a result maintains a higher level of performance), and it also conveys the message of a positive and 'in control' fielding team to the batsman. This can serve to increase the pressure on the batsman, and we know that under increased pressure you are far more likely to make a mistake.

Pressure is further exerted by the whole team committing to the execution of the 'plans' for each ball. So, if the bowler executes their skills effectively and the fielders are in the right place and doing a good job, it should make it more likely that the batsman is going to get out and harder for the batsman to score runs. As we know, as the number of dot balls increases so does the pressure on the batsman.

There are also important aspects of togetherness that impact upon performance when the team is batting. First, the team should have a coherent plan regarding how the team (all eleven batsmen) are going to approach the innings. We know that if each player just plays for themselves then the overall performance might not be great. So, in successful teams each batsman plays their own game but in a way that reflects the overall plan for the team. Good communication between batsmen in the middle and incoming/outgoing batsmen when a wicket has fallen is also important.

In the middle the two batsmen should be looking to encourage and support each other. When a batsman gets out they should look to communicate some clear information to the next batsman when they pass each other as the new batsman is coming in. Many batsmen are just focused on their own frustration when they get out and walk back to the pavilion cursing their bad luck and revisiting the way they got out in their mind. Our advice would be to put that to one side (at least until you get back into the pavilion) and instead quickly think of two or three key points about the pitch, the conditions, or the opposition that will help the incoming batsmen. This team-focused approach could be the difference between the incoming batsman hitting the ground running, or getting out cheaply.

Finally, the support offered by the rest of the team for the two batsmen in the middle is also important. Good, positive, vocal encouragement is always beneficial and can help the players in the middle not be too intimidated by the environment. This idea of a supportive atmosphere is also important, generally in the team, and in training in particular. Where possible the team environment should be a positive one where success is acknowledged and positives are emphasised. The opposite of this is a team environment where players are defensive and trying to focus on reducing the negatives, rather than enhancing the positives. This defensive and negative approach will ultimately have a detrimental effect on performance and confidence.

Another psychological factor that impacts upon the performance of a team is momentum. The phenomenon of momentum is often cited by both players and supporters as a factor that impacts upon performance, and the outcome of games. Momentum is typically thought of as being both an unpredictable and supernatural force outside the control of both individuals and teams, which often dictates the outcomes of competition. Team sports invariably have an ebb and flow, often with one team then another in the ascendency. These periods of good fortune though (referred to as momentum) seem to differ in their length and their frequency.

The gaining of momentum is usually thought of as a factor that can enhance performance while the loss of momentum can be said to have the reverse effect. Recognising that momentum can have a significant effect on team performance and then understanding how to control or to take the momentum in a game is an important skill for any cricket team. Often the momentum in a game will switch based upon a moment of brilliance such as a fantastic catch, or a great stop in the field. These events given more energy and belief to the team, and as such can subconsciously raise the performance level of one team while reducing the energy levels of the other team.

Another important consideration for cricket teams is effective communication. This is required both on and off the pitch to ensure that plans are executed effectively and the whole team knows what is required of them. There are generally three different types of task-focused communication: orientation messages, stimulation messages, and evaluation messages.

Orientation messages are those that encourage the team prior to the start of the game. This could be in the dressing room before going out, or a huddle on the pitch, or alternatively motivational shouts prior to the first ball being bowled.

Stimulation messages occur during performance and are designed to 'gee-up', inspire, and motivate the rest of the team. This role is usually fulfilled by the captain and the wicket keeper, but in the most effective teams is taken up by all of the members of the team.

Evaluation messages are those forms of communication that take place after the game that seek to evaluate the performance, and how the team can move forward in the next game.

Another important consideration relates to how 'important information' is communicated through the team and between the coaching/management staff and the playing staff. In the most effective teams communication structures have been developed that allow each player to communicate their views effectively, and for the coach to be able to communicate effectively with each player. This is often difficult for younger or less experienced players, where confidence to speak up might be lacking. Where any hierarchy exists, the communication will not be equal. This is a concern as research in psychology has shown that the most effective communication, decision-making and planning takes place when all the participants feel they are on the same level, and that all of their views are valid.

While there are always going to be different levels of authority and responsibility in the team, a really effective structure will enable all players to feel they have equal input into the communication process. So, getting different players to say a few words before the game, or leading the 'debrief' after the game is a good way to achieve this.

Chapter 10

Effective communication is underpinned by eight core communication skills:

1. Questioning
2. Reinforcement
3. Reflecting
4. Explaining
5. Listening
6. Humour
7. Laughter
8. Persuasion

Often we are not as effective at communicating as we think. If we first focus on questioning, there are a number of different types of questions which include open or closed questions, leading questions, recall/process questions, probing questions, and rhetorical questions. The essential skill (and what great communicators can just do instinctively) is to ask the right questions at the right time.

Reinforcement is used to convey a positive or negative response following a certain type of behaviour. So, the team offering praise and positive support after a player sprints and dives to stop the ball will increase the likelihood that the player (and the rest of the team) will do the same thing in the future.

Reflecting refers to being empathetic. The more you can reflect the message being communicated (e.g., anger, sadness) the more honest and genuine you will be viewed; this is important to develop if good communication channels are going to be established.

Explaining is another important aspect of communication. The main reason for giving an explanation is to develop the understanding of other players. By doing this you can also ensure learning takes place, clarify ambiguity, help others to learn procedures, reduce anxiety, change attitudes and improve your own understanding.

There are three specific types of explaining: interpretative, descriptive, and reason-giving. Interpretative explanations address the question "What?" These explanations seek to clarify an issue or specify the central meaning of a term or statement. Descriptive explanations address the question "How?" describing processes, structures and procedures. Reason-giving explanations address the question "Why?" They involve reasons based on principles or generalizations, motives, obligations, or values.

Probably the most important communication skill (and the least well developed in many people) is the ability to listen. In a communication sense, listening is the ability to understand and process information. The listener must take care to pay attention to the speaker fully, and then repeat, in the listener's own words. A common error in conversations relates to people not listening fully. Instead of listening to what the other person is saying many people take the opportunity to plan what they are going to say next. In such cases important information can be missed, and you might both end up having different conversations.

Humour and laughter are also very important aspects of communication. Everyday conversation thrives on wordplay, sarcasm, anecdotes, jokes, and banter. These help to break the ice, fill uncomfortable pauses, negotiate requests for favours, and build group solidarity. Humour, above all else, is a shared experience; indeed in team-focused situations there are few more useful social skills than humour. In particular humour might be used to achieve the following:

- Search for information
- Give information
- Exert interpersonal control
- Be used for group control
- Manage anxiety

Laughter, while often linked to humour, is not necessarily linked explicitly. There are different types of laughter that serve different functions including:

- Humorous laughter
- Social laughter
- Ignorance laughter
- Evasion laughter
- Apologetic laughter
- Anxious laughter
- Derisory laughter

- Joyous laughter

Laughter can be used to try to project dignity and control when experiencing stress or anxiety (anxious laughter), or might be used to cover up the fact that you do not know the answer to a particular question (ignorance laughter). Equally social laughter can be used to create positive feelings and emotions in the recipient.

The final important communication skill is persuasion. Skilled persuaders are experts in adapting their message to those groups that they seek to influence. This adaptation is achieved in the following way. First, to identify current obstacles to agreement or compliance (these obstacles are, in essence, the basis for the individual's resistance). Second, to construct effective messages to remove or minimize these obstacles that are underpinning the individual's resistance.

Communication in cricket teams is strongly affected by the type of leader (coach or manager) who is in the position of authority. As a result communication has been highlighted as the key vehicle for effective coaching. The crucial foundation for effective communication for the cricket coach is their credibility, the degree of trust, and mutual respect that exists.

Research in sport psychology suggests that players will be more motivated by a coach whom they have a lot of respect for. Coaches who are good communicators are good at explaining, clarifying, and individualizing instructions to meet the needs of the individual player.

Building a Better Team

A crucial aspect of any successful team is the degree to which each player clearly understands their job/role in the team. Confusion in different people's understanding of a role can be crippling to the team. As a result there are a number of steps the communicator needs to take.

First, the captain or the coach needs to clearly *communicate* what each player's role in the team entails. Second, the captain or coach needs to check that each player *understands* what their role is in the team. Linked to this should be a discussion of what the coach/captain would expect to see from the player in fulfilling this role (essentially what behaviours are required).

The coach might tell his opening batsman that his role is to score quickly. In the coach's mind this could be rotating the strike, and taking at least a single off each ball by playing low risk shots. The opening batsman given the message to score quickly might set about trying to hit every ball out of the park and achieving this by selecting high risk shot options. So, while the player and the coach agree on the role, they have very different views on the behaviours and actions required to fulfil that role. Once this has been clarified, it is also important to get the player to accept this role in the team and the associated behaviours. The player might not feel that it is the best way for them to play, but the coach/captain needs to explain how this will contribute to team success and as a result look to get the player to 'buy-in' to the role.

The next step is then for the coach to communicate the role and required behaviours to the rest of the team. The coach and opening batsman could be clear regarding what his role is, and the actions that are required to fulfil the role, but the rest of the team might have a different understanding of what the role should be. If this is the case, the team could become less positive and supportive as they feel that the player is not doing what is required for the team. So, it is also important that each member of the team has a clear understanding of what *everyone's role* is in the team, and what actions/behaviours are associated with the successful completion of these roles.

Another important aspect of developing a successful team is developing something called 'shared mental models'. Shared mental models refer to an organised understanding of the game, the team's tactics, and the way to play, that is shared by a team. This sharing of knowledge is seen to enhance the team's understanding of each other's views and needs.

Shared knowledge then leads to more efficient coordination as the team can anticipate each other's actions. This generally involves knowledge about the equipment used by the team, understanding the team's goals and requirements to perform well, awareness of the strengths and weaknesses of their teammates (skills, habits, beliefs, etc), and what the team views as acceptable behaviour and approaches.

Chapter 10

Team effectiveness will improve if team members have a shared understanding of the task, team, equipment, and situation. So building on this assumption, the greater the degree of shared understanding, the greater the potential benefits. One example of this was the approach adopted by the ex-England Soccer manager Sven-Goran Erikkson and his sport psychologist Willi Railo. Erikkson and Railo targeted specific players within the team to act as 'cultural architects' through which the shared mental model could be developed. The players selected had developed a good grasp of what was required and it was their understanding of the management's plans that was used to influence the understanding of their teammates.

Another way in which you can forge an effective and more 'together' team is through facilitating the individuals in the team to get to know each other better. So, an important aspect of many teams is that they socialise together. The more you get to know someone the more likely you are to try and succeed on their behalf. A group of strangers will work for themselves and not for the team.

The England team, before heading to Australia for the Ashes series in 2010/11, adopted this approach. England had not won a series in Australia for over 20 years before the tour. The team management recognised that there would be significant hardship and challenges for the players over the duration of the tour so decided that getting the players to know each other, and as a result fight for each other, would be a good step to take. So, the England management team planned a team building camp in Bavaria, Southern Germany.

The camp was composed of both physical and mental challenges such as hiking and abseiling. The specifics of the camp were kept secret from the players beforehand, and the players even had to leave their mobile phones behind. As well as the physical challenges the team also learned more about making decisions under pressure, leadership, and the factors that contribute to team success.

The camp also involved mutual sharing activities around the campfire, all of which sought to enhance team cohesion. The (then) England Captain Andrew Strauss was impressed with the experience stating that *"It was a tough but rewarding five days and I know every player has gained greater insight into themselves, their own team environment and environments outside cricket."*

At the time the media were less convinced suggesting it would have been more important for the players to rest ahead of the winter tour to Australia; particularly when it emerged that one of England's key bowlers, Jimmy Anderson, suffered a cracked rib after participating in the activities. However, England did go on to win the Ashes series and a number of the players and support staff cited the camp in Germany as helping them to become a closer and more united team.

Finally, developing collective confidence in the team is also crucial. Collective confidence relates to the degree to which the team thinks they will be successful. In sport psychology this is referred to as collective efficacy. Collective confidence is important because it influences what players choose to do as team members.

Collective confidence beliefs effect team behaviours, such as the tactics the team chooses to use, the level of effort that the team puts into the game, and the extent to which the team will persist when faced with challenges.

While performance-orientated outcomes are the most important factors associated with collective confidence, beliefs regarding team functioning also contribute to group thought patterns. The higher the team feels their collective confidence is, the higher the team's motivational investment in their performance, the stronger their staying power in the face of setbacks, and the greater their overall levels of performance.

Research has shown that the most important factor contributing to each player's beliefs about team functioning is previous experience. Cricket teams that experience success in a specific form of the game, or situation, have an expectation that they will perform equally well in future tasks of a similar nature. If a team outperforms an opponent the first time that they play, the team will have a higher level of confidence that they can do the same in future contests against similar competition. Conversely, teams that suffer performance setbacks will lack confidence in their abilities to succeed in subsequent games.

Watching a team that is similar in performance ability can also help to increase the team's level of confidence to succeed in similar situations. So, a mid-table cricket team seeing another mid-table cricket team beating the team that is top of the league will lead to greater confidence that they can do the same thing. Similarly, seeing a team who are at a similar level to yourself struggle, undermines the observing team's level of collective confidence.

The provision of feedback is another way collective confidence can be altered. Feedback that conveys information about the team's capabilities will likely have the most influence on beliefs of collective confidence. Spectator and media support can also impact upon the collective confidence of the team. It seems pretty logical, but it is true that teams who hear applause and positive support have greater collective confidence compared to teams who experience jeers and abuse, or negative reviews in the media. This is important because teams high in collective confidence feel more in control, and as a result, have less reason to worry or falter under pressure.

Cricket players communicate in a number of specific settings including training, before the game, during the game, after the game, and socially. However, communication during the game can become problematic due to the requirements of a number of competing task demands. Effective communication is apparent when team members listen to one another and attempt to build on each other's contributions. The way that the team communicates can be enhanced by doing the following:

1. Make sure everyone is pulling in the same direction (wants to achieve the same things). Make sure the team is aware of, and agrees with, the team's goals.
2. Openly discuss strategies to enhance team harmony, and for team members to support each other better both inside and outside of the sporting environment. As part of the planning process, during the pre-season period, is a good time to implement this.
3. Listen to what other people have to say (they are then more likely to listen to you). Actually listen to, process, and discuss other options and views.
4. Learn how to give and receive feedback constructively. This is a skill that can be learnt and improved.
5. Learn how to tolerate each other better (accepting each individual for who they are). Players need the opportunity to resolve issues and differences.

6. Avoid backstabbing and gossiping about other teammates. This leads to a divided dressing room, confrontation, a negative environment and a decrease in effort.
7. Keep confrontation private. Deal with issues directly with the other person. Once issues are public, individuals feel they need to 'act' a role to not lose face as well as resolve the issue.
8. Recognize that not all conflicts can be resolved, but can be managed. You could have two players in the team that don't get on, but who want to achieve the same thing, so in performance and training environments put their differences aside.

Summary

In the modern game, developing an effective team is crucial to success. Sometimes successful teams just develop, but a strategy that relies on this 'chance' development is a little risky. A more effective approach is deliberately looking to build a team that can be effective both on and off the pitch.

There are a number of relatively easy steps that can be taken to enhance the probability that your cricket team will be successful. The most important of which is to have a clear understanding of what success will look like for the team. Success can be achieved by identifying clear goals and targets for your team. Coupled to this is the importance of players knowing what they are supposed to be doing in the team - to help the group achieve its goals and targets. As such each player having a well-communicated understanding of what the coach/captain expects of them is important for success.

Once the team is clear on what success will be for the team - the next step is to put in place the plans and processes to work towards achieving these goals.

Key messages:

- Time should be spent focusing on building an effective team
- Players understanding their role in the team is very important
- The quality of communication in a team will impact upon performance

- There is a link between the togetherness of the team and performance
- Involve all of the team in planning activities such as team goal setting

Further reading:

Carron, A. V., Hausenblas, H. A., & Eys, M. A. (2005). *Group dynamics in sport* (3rd ed.). Morgantown: Fitness Information Technology.

Cotterill, S. T. (2012). *Team psychology in sports: Theory and practice.* Abingdon: Routledge.

Advanced reading:

Paradis, K. F., & Martin, L. J. (2012). Team building in sport: Linking theory and research to practical application. *Journal of Sport Psychology in Action, 3*(3), 159-170.

11

Effective Decision Making

"The great thing in hitting is, not to be half-hearted about it; but when you make up your mind to hit, to do it as if the whole match depended upon that particular stroke." W. G. Grace

"One of the great thrills of bowling is planning the dismissals of batsmen."
Kapil Dev

"The hallmark of a great captain is the ability to win the toss at the right time." Richie Benaud

Cricket is all about making the right decisions at the right time. Whether you are the captain, a batsman, a bowler, or the coach you have to make important decisions all the time. Then crucially you need to commit to your decision 100%.

The captain and coach have to decide who the best 'team' of players are to play on any given day in any given match. Also the captain needs to make a decision on whether to bat or field first, specific field placings, and when to make bowling changes.

The bowler needs to make decisions on what field they would like, which variation they are looking to bowl, and what they think the batsman is going to do.

For the batsman it is really about which stroke you are going to play. Can you make the right decision at the right time? Part of this process relates to how you make decisions (Are you decisive?), also past experience is important (Have you had to make these decisions before?), finally the knowledge you have is also important (What evidence have you got to support your decisions?).

All of these different types of decisions take different amounts of time and effort. From the captain who has quite a lot of time to consider the conditions in the morning and what they will do (if they win the toss), to the batsman facing the fast bowler who needs to make an instant decision on what shot to play (or to get out of the way of the ball).

The speed at which you can change your decision when required is also an important factor in cricket. If you just play or bowl premeditated plans then there is always the possibility that you will get it wrong. Thinking 'I am going to hit this for a six' without knowing where the ball is going is a dangerous strategy (although there are some times in a match when you have to do this).

If you understand how you make decisions, what factors impact upon these decisions, and how to make decisions under pressure, you can further enhance your performance. At the death in a T20 game both the bowler and batsman need to think clearly and make quick, decisive, and effective decisions for each delivery. This chapter will explore this skill of decision making in greater detail, the impact it has upon your cricketing performance, and crucially how to get better at it.

What is Decision-Making?

In general terms decision-making can be viewed as the process of committing to a particular course of action (choosing one option over another).

More specific definitions of decision-making have been suggested including 'the selection of one option from a set of two or more options'. Very simply though, decision-making relates to the choices that you make when there are a number of available options to choose from. For example, a captain has two choices at the toss (if they win the toss). Either to bat first, or to bowl first. On the face of it this is a simple decision, there are only two choices. There are a number of factors that will influence this decision, but it is a choice between two options.

For a batsman facing a bowler there could be a number of different choices that the player could make. In all cases these decisions are influenced by past experience and their knowledge of the specific situation they are in. It is also important to recognise that there is very rarely a cut and dried 'right' decision. For example the right shot to play to a particular bowler depends upon the strengths and skills of the batsman. If you are very good at playing the short ball the right decision to a ball at chest height might be the pull shot. Whereas if you are not particularly good at the pull shot the right decision might be to get out of the way of the ball.

So, past experience and knowledge have an effect on what the right decision for that player in any situation should be. Taking the example of the captain suggested earlier, they have two choices at the toss to either bat or to field. This decision will be based on past *experience* (Do the team win or lose more when batting first or second? Do teams batting first or second usually win on this pitch? Is it better to set a target or to chase one down?). The decision will also be based on the *knowledge* the captain has (knowing the impact of the playing conditions on both batting and bowling performance, what the weather forecast is, the physical condition of the team, the strengths of the opposition). So the more knowledge and experience the captain has, the more able they should be in making a decision.

A similar thought process also exists for a batsman waiting for the next delivery. They make their decisions about what shots to play based on their past experience and personal knowledge. Past experience will relate to what shots are more (or less) successful for that player. Also, knowledge regarding the impact that the conditions can have, and what variations the bowler usually uses will also impact upon the decision.

There is one other important source of information that allows you to make a decision when batting. It is the information that you pick up from the bowler when they are running in (e.g., position of the ball, hand position, angle of run-in to the crease) that allows you to 'pick' the delivery before it is bowled. If you are able to do this, making the right decision is much easier. Unfortunately, this type of decision-making is automatic, in that you don't have time to consciously think about it. Which is a problem because if you are not actively thinking about it - can you practice how to make the right decision?

This is even more of an issue when facing fast bowlers, as research has shown that if you wait until the bowler releases the ball to make your decision - your brain does not have enough time to activate the relevant response before the ball is past you. In these cases the batsman needs to have decided what shot they are going to play before the bowler has finished their bowling action. So in effect the batsman has to try to 'anticipate' what the bowler is going to do before they do it. The quicker the bowler, the earlier in the action the appropriate decision needs to be made. So, anything that you can pick up from the bowler before they release the ball could be crucial to making the right decision.

Bowlers also need to make clear decisions regarding what tactical plans they are going to use and what sequence of deliveries they are going to play (the way they construct their over to the batsman). The ability to make clear decisions regarding the tactics they are going to employ is a crucial aspect of successful bowling. Linked to this, though, is whether the bowler can then execute the relevant skills.

So decision making in cricket involves the ability to make the right call (the right decision) and to be able to execute the relevant skills confidently. One bowler who was excellent at both of these was Australian leg spinning legend Shane Warne. Warne had both of these skills in abundance. When talking about Warne in 2006, the then Australian captain Ricky Ponting highlighted that Warne's ability to think about the game and to set batsmen up amazed him. In particular Ponting referred to an instance during the tea interval at the Oval during the Ashes test in 2005. Ponting recounted that "*He told me how an entire over against Kevin Pietersen was going to unfold. He said to me 'I'm going to start around the wicket for the first three balls, bowl them way outside leg stump and he'll pad up to every one of them'. Then he said 'I'll go back over the wicket fourth and fifth ball, bowl him a slow loopy leg spinner that pitches outside off stump that he'll try and slog-sweep over mid-wicket, and he'll miss it'. And that's what happened.*"

Ian Healy the Australian wicket keeper also highlighted Warne's ability to execute his skills effectively as well. Healey reflected that "*He was the only leg spinner I knew who could so definitely change his plans within one ball, he could do it immediately and definitely.*" So bowlers need to be able to make bigger tactical decisions as well as ball-by-ball decisions.

The Effects of Decision-Making on Cricket Performance

Very simply, better decision-making makes you a better and more successful player. The more often you make the right decision the more often you are able to execute your skills effectively. If you make poor decisions, or don't fully commit to the decisions you make, your likelihood of being effective is significantly reduced.

If, as a batsman, you make the right decision regarding the shot you select, then you are more likely to be in control of that period of play. As a captain if you make the right decision regarding batting or fielding, and the conditions you are faced with are favourable, you increase the likelihood of your team winning the game. As a bowler, if you make the correct decisions regarding which delivery to bowl then you are more likely to win the battle with the batsman. In all cases making the right decision is advantageous to your performance. Being able to make the right decision, and then execute it under pressure is the *ultimate aim* of any sports performer. This skill of decision-making is one of the factors that ultimately determines those who are successful and those who are not.

There are a number of factors that can impact upon your ability to make the right decision when playing cricket. As mentioned, knowledge and past experience are important factors, if you don't have one (or both) your ability to make the right decisions consistently is reduced. Also, the situation that you are playing in can have an effect. Most of us are okay at making decisions when there is no pressure. So, in practice, it is easy to make the right call. But under pressure this gets far more difficult to do effectively. This is for two main reasons.

First, under pressure (where there is an important outcome, like winning) the consequences of making the wrong decision are significantly greater (see also the *Performing Under Pressure Chapter*). If you step down the wicket in the nets and miss the ball as a batsman, you just move on to the next ball. In a game if you do this you get stumped and lose your wicket. As a result, making an effective decision is made more difficult due to the greater consequences involved.

Chapter 11

Psychological factors can also have an effect on your ability to make an effective decision. So when a player becomes overly emotional their ability to think clearly is reduced. This means that you are no longer able to consider the different options available to you and make a good, appropriate, decision. Also, as you get more emotional you find it more difficult to focus and become more distracted; this again stops you from making good decisions (as you might be thinking about the wrong things). As a result, you start missing important bits of information (such as changes in field placings) and end up playing the ball straight to the recently moved fielder.

Players who do well and make the right decisions under pressure are those players who can continue to think clearly and not get distracted by their emotions. Tiredness and dehydration can also reduce your ability to make good decisions, which is another reason why being physically fit and fully hydrated are now important aspects of cricket.

The opposition might also look to hide or 'keep' important information from you. One example of this could be the bowler shielding the ball so you can't see the seam position, or the batsman making false movements to try and get the bowler to select a certain delivery the batsman would prefer, or fielders changing position once the bowler is running in.

Spinners are masters at trying to conceal the delivery they are about to bowl. One of the reasons for this relates back to a point made previously in this chapter. With fast bowlers once the ball has been released you do not have sufficient time to make a decision, so you have to anticipate what is going to happen. With spinners you still have enough time to start moving, so spinners look to hide and deceive the batsman. This is both in terms of the type of delivery and the pace at which the ball is delivered. Pace is an important factor as we can only really make a call on this when the ball has left the bowlers hand; by the time we have seen enough of the flight 'to be sure' we already need to have started our movements. This, in part, explains how batsmen can be deceived 'in flight' by the spinners.

Traditionally, emotion has been thought to have a negative impact on a cricketer's ability to make good decisions under pressure. However, research in psychology has revealed that emotions can be an indispensable part of good decision-making and that emotions are critical to making the right decisions. This is because people rely on somatic (physical) markers such as *physiological responses* to situations of gain or loss to make value relevant decisions.

So, in the heat of battle, decisions are not simply made based on cool reason but also by how people feel. From this view, certain physiological signals serve as warning signals from the body for unfavourable decisions. Although players may not have conscious awareness of such warning signals from their body, the generation of these anticipatory signals has been shown to reduce the selection of risky or unfavourable options.

There is also a link between stress/anxiety and decision-making. Evidence suggests that as we become more stressed or anxious it takes us longer to make a decision. This is probably linked to the idea of a fixed thinking space in the brain. As we become more stressed we use more of this thinking space, which leaves less for us to execute our skills (see *Chapter Three* for further details of mental capacity).

Another factor that is worth considering when discussing decision-making is the idea of risk taking. Whenever you make a decision (in a situation where there is more than one option) there is always a risk that you might not be making the right choice. Sometimes the risks and associated rewards linked with certain decisions become important to understanding the decisions that are made. Often players are faced with a decision between two options of varying risk. In these types of situations the players make two main judgments. The first relates to the potential *rewards* attached to each decision, and the second relates to the associated *consequences* with that course of action.

The classic example of this in cricket is a batsman who goes for a high-risk but high reward shot (consequence is an increased likelihood of getting out by playing the ball in the air, reward is six runs) to score a six, at the expense of a low risk but relatively low reward shot for two runs (playing the ball along the ground).

The context of the game will be one factor that impacts upon the decision that the batsman takes, depending on the state of the game and the point in the game that the decision is taken. However, alongside this there are also differences between different players regarding the degree to which they are willing to take a risk.

Chapter 11

Players who happily take risks are generally focused on the rewards associated with the risk, while players who are averse to taking risks generally focus on the consequences of failing to execute that course of action correctly. Ideally, we are looking for a balance between the two.

When it comes to understanding decision-making behaviour it is important to understand the situation, the skills of the particular player, and also to understand the risk taking character of the players. These differences in the underlying character of a player can be seen in the way that they act.

Some players are very good at making cool, deliberate and calculated decisions, while other players are more likely to make hot and emotive decisions. There is also one other important point when considering risk-taking behaviour and this relates to the perspective from which the 'risk' is viewed.

A player's perception of the level of risk in a given game situation depends on the ability of the individual player. If a player is not very good at the hook shot, then playing the hook shot is taking a risk. Whereas if a player is very accomplished at playing the hook shot it becomes a significantly less risky option. One example of this is the 'switch hit' executed successfully by Kevin Pietersen. For most players this would be a very risky shot, but because he has spent a significant amount of time practicing the shot it has become a relatively low-risk option for him.

So, it is important to recognize that there are individual differences. What is risky for one person is not necessarily risky for another. If you want to truly understand whether a player is taking a risk or not you need to know what their strengths are. Indeed, if they are playing to their strengths they are choosing their low-risk option. This strengths-focused approach reduces the associated risk, but also increases the likelihood that they will make a good decision and execute it effectively and quickly.

There is also a significant link between decision-making and confidence. This link works in both directions. First, effective decision-making experiences increase your confidence (see also *Chapter Six* on *Playing Confidently*). If you have previously made good decisions the next time you are in a similar situation you will believe that you can do what is required; as a result this increases your confidence further, which in turn increases the likelihood of success. The more a batsman is able to pick what a specific player is bowling at them the more likely they are to feel confident the next time they play that particular player.

The second link relates to the impact that confidence can have on your decision-making. The more confident you feel the more you are likely to make a decision and then execute it effectively. If you are lacking confidence there is more likely to be self-doubt. This self-doubt has the effect of slightly delaying the decision you make or stops you committing fully to that course of action. This in turn means it takes slightly longer to execute the course of action you have chosen. This delay can be the difference between having good timing or your timing being slightly off. This can then determine how well you execute your skills.

Enhancing Decision-Making

Let us now examine the factors that determine decision-making ability. We will start by looking at the knowledge you hold that helps you to make a decision.

A key component of knowledge is past experience. Past experience is one of those things that, as the name suggests, you only really get through playing lots of cricket. If you have faced the same player 20 times previously you will have a better idea of how to play them than if it was the first time. Also, it is not just your past experience but also the degree of success that you have enjoyed that is important. If this player had taken your wicket on many occasions previously, or possibly scored a lot of runs, this can have a negative effect on your ability to make the most effective decisions against them.

It is not a coincidence that when Shane Warne was still playing for Australia Kevin Pietersen became very effective at both picking and playing his deliveries. Warne and Pietersen, at the time, had been playing county cricket together for Hampshire County Cricket Club. As a result, Pietersen would have spent far more time facings Warne's deliveries than could be expected for most international players. This exposure to Warne's game developed Pietersen's ability to pick his deliveries, and as a result this increased his confidence when playing against him. Both of these factors enabled Pietersen to make good, early decisions regarding how to play the deliveries he faced. All of which contributed to his increased success rate.

So, knowledge is partially composed of past experiences, but it can also come from other sources. One great source is other people (current players, ex-players, coaches, and officials). Asking an experienced captain about what decisions to make (and *why*) can help you to become a better captain even if you have not captained many games. In the same way getting tips from other players on the best thing to do in a certain situation, or against a certain player, is also very useful. As the captain you don't need to have all the answers, but you need to know where to get them!

When you face a player (batsman or bowler), or even a specific type of player (e.g., leg spinner) your body starts to store information about what they do, and how they do it. For batsmen facing bowlers this relates to the way the bowler holds the ball, how they run in, the angle into the crease, their limb position (and so on). For bowlers this relates to the batsman's position in the crease, their body alignment, the way they hold the bat, their head position and the transfer of their weight, amongst others things.

This store of information is where your ability to 'read' the game is developed. The more exposure you have to specific players the better you become at facing them. The implication here is that you need to practice as much as possible in the real environment against real players to develop this ability to 'know' what is coming next.

The recognition of stored signals happens at a sub-conscious level. You don't have the time to react fully once the bowler has released the ball (particularly for quick bowlers), you need to make a best guess based on the knowledge and information you have. To achieve this your brain takes the visual signals you are receiving and checks them against those stored in your memory to see if there is a match that can then tell you what is about to happen. The better the store, the more likely there is to be a match, and this in turn increases the speed and accuracy of the decision, which then makes it more likely that you are going to be successful.

In the case of a bowler the more variations they have the more information you need, to make an effective decision, so the harder it becomes to make the right decision. Also, if you need to know what cues relate to a certain delivery the bowler can use this knowledge to their advantage. If the give-away clue is the position of the ball in the hand, hiding the ball with the other hand when running in can make it far more difficult for the batsman to make the right decision.

All this has implications for practice. You need to be clear what you are trying to practice and develop. To get better at decision-making you need to practice for it. Facing a bowling machine is not going to help a batsman to 'pick' the ball the bowler is delivering. So this in turn should influence the design and delivery of the sessions you are involved in.

If you are looking to practice decision-making then you need to make the task as realistic as possible. So, facing real bowlers on a real pitch is the best option for a batsman. Using bowling machines is great for honing your technical skills, but not great for helping the development of decision-making skills. This is predominantly for two main reasons. First, the bowling machine lacks spontaneous variability and a brain. The bowling machine is very good at putting the ball in a certain spot at a certain speed, but this doesn't reflect the true demands of the game where the bowler can change what and where they bowl. So, with a bowling machine you can get very good at executing a specific shot when the ball is in a specific location, but not develop the ability to know *when* the ball is going to be there.

Second, batsmen pick up important information from the bowler when they run in. This might be from the position of the seam, the way the bowler is holding the ball, or the position of the bowler's elbow. It is differences in this information that allow the batsman to start to be able to distinguish between different types of delivery. If you remove that information, the batsman does not develop the required skills to effectively 'pick' what the bowler is bowling.

To practice decision-making where quick reactions are crucial you need to practice in a similar environment. Ideally this should happen out in the middle facing a full fielding team. While this might not be achievable, most of the time, there needs to be an understanding that every change from this (e.g., number of fielders, location of practice, etc.) reduces the ability of players to develop their decision-making skills. This can be a particular challenge in countries where the weather conditions mean cricket has to be played indoors for part of the year.

Other types of decision-making can be developed and practised in different ways. While it is important for a captain and bowler to make decisions regarding field placings and bowling plans in game situations, these more conscious decisions can also be developed outside of the game environment. These types of decisions are underpinned by significant tactical knowledge and can be developed through conversations with other players, coaches, and captains. This knowledge can also be developed by watching others making these decisions and trying to understand *how/why* they made the decisions they did. Just as importantly, would you have done the same things in a given situation? Why?

Until recently it was assumed that to develop elite performance levels in cricket - many years of hands-on experience were needed. It turns out, however, that amassing experience does not necessarily lead to expert levels of performance.

Many experts now argue that trying to train and improve decision-making in a player may be far more beneficial in comparison to simply gaining more game experience. While we are not saying that accumulating this experience is unimportant, there is a recognition that decision-making training can help to 'fast track' players to be effective at a higher level. In particular, developing your ability to select the 'right information to focus on' should greatly improve your ability to make good decisions under pressure.

The use of video footage has also been suggested as a way to improve decision-making. Whilst you might not be able to practice facing a specific bowler you can at least watch video footage of them to get used to watching them and picking up the relevant visual cues - to anticipate what they are going to bowl. This is further enhanced by having the knowledge of results (the outcome), and being able to view the approach when a slow ball is bowled. This footage could then be contrasted with video of a different type of delivery. It is important to clarify that you are not trying to 'freeze-frame' the different footage to try and consciously identify what the differences are. The chances are that you wouldn't really be successful; even if you were - it might not really help. What is important is to process the visual information at a sub-conscious level and then allow your brain to experience the scenario without having to really 'be in the situation'. In an ideal world, you would also view this footage on a big screen (where the bowler ends up almost life-sized). This life-size approach and perspective is far more relevant for the brain to make associations.

Finally, you might look to develop your risk taking. There are two specific aspects to this. The first relates to the degree to which the option *actually is risky*. Playing a shot in the air might be a risky shot, but if you have practiced and practiced and can clear the rope with ease 10 times out of 10, this makes it a lower risk shot (it might look risky to someone else but it is not that risky for you).

The second way in which you can develop your risk taking is to develop a better understanding of the rewards and the consequences associated with different courses of action. Often players will say 'I didn't think about that' when asked why they chose a particular option. So having a good discussion with your coach about the merits (and drawbacks) of certain shots, deliveries, or passages of play further enhances your knowledgebase from which you can then make decisions.

Summary

Cricket is all about effective decision-making. Whether it is the anticipation of the batsman or bowler in the heat of battle, or the deliberate decision-making of the captain or coach regarding tactics – the sport hinges on effective decision-making.

Like any other skill, decision-making can be trained and developed. Often cricketers just let their decision-making ability develop over time as they accumulate more experience, but this development can be accelerated with clearly structured and focused development work in the right environment.

Most players don't really stop and think about how they make decisions in their game. But, if they did, they would be half-way-there in knowing how to practice to improve.

Chapter 11

The risks associated with different decisions should be fully understood if you are going to make the most effective decisions in specific situations. Coaches, and other experts, can help you to develop your own knowledgebase so when it comes to making a potentially risky decision, in a game, you do so whilst fully understanding the associated risks and rewards.

Key messages:

- When you make a decision you commit to a specific course of action
- Often in cricket you have to anticipate rather than wait to make a decision
- The better your decision-making the more success you will have as a player
- Both knowledge and experience significantly increase decision-making
- You can 'fast track' your development by practicing for decision-making in a realistic environment that mirrors the real thing

Further reading:

Bar-Eli, M., Plessner, H., & Raab, M. (2011). *Judgement, decision making and success in sport*. Chichester: Wiley-Blackwell.

Advanced reading:

Muller, S., Abernethy, B., & Farrow, D. (2006). How do world-class cricket batsmen anticipate a bowler's intention? *The Quarterly Journal of Experimental Psychology, 59*(12), 2162-2186.

Phillips, E. J., Davids, K.W., Renshaw, I., & Portus M. (2010). The development of fast bowling experts in Australian cricket. *Talent Development and Excellence*, 137-148.

End of Play

In this book we have provided expert and contemporary advice on a number of pertinent aspects relative to success in cricket. In essence, we have tried to cover the fundamental areas which, according to theory and evidence, can make a difference to players and teams.

Within this book we have demonstrated the clear link between psychology and success in cricket through illustrations of some of the world's best players. Along the way we have outlined the importance of:

- Confidence
- How to control emotions
- Ways to increase concentration
- How to become more mentally tough
- How to build a successful team
- Effective leadership and decision making
- Dealing with pressure
- Staying motivated

In addition, we have presented a number of suggestions, techniques, and mental skills which can be used to foster a more effective mindset and approach to playing and dealing with the demands of cricket. We hope that readers will find these informative and useful.

There is nothing magic about sport psychology and therefore mental skills are like physical skills and take time and practice to master and develop. To illustrate, for some players, perfecting the effective use of imagery can take many years. Therefore, we ask that readers are patient with their own expectations upon reading this book.

Developing an appropriate mindset, necessary for success in cricket, is a skill in itself and therefore commitment, motivation, and patience should be offered accordingly. Through the development of an appropriate mindset, it is likely that players will endure much more confidence, consistency, enjoyment, and success and become champions in their cricket.

End of Play

Champion cricketers think smart at all times. They think clearly, decisively, and rationally when under pressure. They do not dwell on the past or become transfixed by the future. They are masters of staying in the now; staying in the moment.

Champions have unshakeable belief in their ability to be successful. They believe that the impossible is possible, they work hard, and remain persistent. They act confident at all times through positive body language.

Champions use their mental energy effectively. They learn to preserve the precious reservoir which permits effective concentration through the development and use of effective routines.

Champions are committed. They set goals which challenge, excite, and energise them. They never rest on their laurels but also look to stay ahead of the rest.

Champions know themselves intimately. They understand their emotions and how emotions can affect their performance.

Champion teams provide support, encouragement, and confidence to each other. They are have clearly defined roles, pathways of communication, and share the same performance goals.

Champion teams behave like champion teams. They never give in, work hard at all times, and persist in getting things correct. They win well, and never lose without giving their all.

In our opinion, psychology is common sense which people (including cricketers) either ignore or forget. Thinking positively, staying calm, remaining focused, and believing in one's ability are thoughts and feelings which all players should engage in during practice and competition. However, the reality is that very few do these things on a regular basis with the required success. Therefore, we encourage players and coaches to dedicate regular time to the development of successful mindsets using some of the tips and strategies included within this book.

We hope that *The Psychology of Cricket* has changed, and will continue to change, how you think, feel, and behave about your cricket, and thus allow you fulfil your potential and become a champion cricketer!

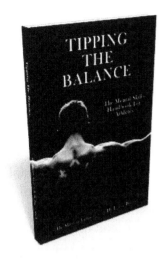

Tipping The Balance: The Mental Skills Handbook For Athletes by Dr Martin Turner & Dr Jamie Barker

Many athletes grow up with the philosophy that their mental approach to performance is fixed. They do the same things over and over again and expect excellence. But we know that mental approaches are not fixed. They are extremely changeable and adaptable, and therefore the greatest athletes can develop their mental approaches to fulfil their potential. Athletes who can deal with pressure enjoy their sport more, achieve excellence and are resilient to the demands of competition and training.

Tipping The Balance offers contemporary evidence-based and highly practical mental strategies that help an athlete to develop the crucial mental skills that enable them to thrive under pressure, perform consistently when it matters most, and enjoy the challenge of the big event.

This book is about empowering you - the athlete - no matter what level you perform at. In this book you will discover the secrets of how the world's greatest athletes draw on cutting edge psychological skills to use what's between their ears to maximize performance.

Tipping The Balance is the sister book to *What Business Can Learn From Sport Psychology: Ten Lessons for Peak Professional Performance*

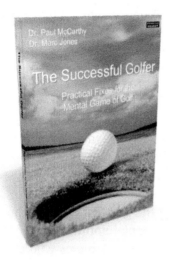

The Successful Golfer: Practical Fixes for the Mental Game of Golf by Dr Paul McCarthy & Dr Marc Jones

You do not have to play many rounds of golf to understand how much of the game is played in the mind. Different courses, conditions, and shot requirements all present unique challenges that need focus and mental strength from the winning player. In turn, moving from the practice range onto the golf course can often magically produce drops in concentration, increased frustration, and unexpected self-doubt: drives go wayward, three foot putts get missed, and water features seem to become magnets.

The Successful Golfer is designed to help address 50 of the most common faults that players experience and which hold them back. These include: hitting the self-destruct button when winning, nervousness on the first tee, lost confidence, failing to practise as you play, losing focus off poor drives, and many more. Each fault is remedied with a clear practical fix. You will learn to develop effective practice plans, build a dependable pre-shot routine, cope with the pressures of competitive golf, and deal with distractions.

In the second part of the book, lessons from 30 fascinating research studies on golf are presented to help keep you ahead of the field. They include research on putting, practice, choking, and overthinking. In the third and final part of the book, clear instructions are provided on developing a number of highly effective techniques that can be used across a wide variety of situations. These include: pre-shot routines, breathing exercises, goal setting, and how best to practice.

Lightning Source UK Ltd.
Milton Keynes UK
UKOW05f1001040517
300476UK00017B/541/P